women runners

women runners

stories of transformation

Edited by
IRENE RETI
and
BETTIANNE SHONEY SIEN

BREAKAWAY BOOKS
HALCOTTSVILLE, NEW YORK
2001

WOMEN RUNNERS: Stories of Transformation

ISBN: 1-891369-25-3
Library of Congress Catalog Card Number: 2001088408

Published by Breakaway Books
P.O. Box 24
Halcottsville, NY 12438
(800) 548-4348
www.breakawaybooks.com

Breakaway Books are distributed to the trade by Consortium

FIRST EDITION

women runners

Aida K. Press

Rachel Running

for my eight-year-old granddaughter

Like an Olympic runner
hunched down
left leg stretched behind you
head up
at the sound of the gun
you're off
long legs pumping
like pistons
elbows slicing the air
brown hair flying.

Run, Rachel, run
for your foremothers
hampered by corsets
and long skirts
for women today
hobbled by high heels
for Chinese women

with bound feet
and Muslim women
shrouded in veils.
Run for all of us
who never dared to run
and for those who tried
but were banned from the race.
Run for Congress
run for President
run for the prize.
If you win
or lose
you win.

When she started running in her early fifties, Aida K. Press felt air-
borne. Now that she is a septuagenarian, she has returned to earth, con-
tenting herself with fast walking and watching the Boston Marathon.
Since retiring as editor of the Radcliffe Quarterly *and director of pub-*
lic information at Radcliffe, she has been writing poems and articles.

Alison Townsend

Going the Distance

I.

There comes a time late in the afternoon when the light is just so and my circadian rhythms are at exactly a certain point, when the only solid thought in my mind is to *run*. To change into my baggy shorts and faded Berkeley tank top with the rainbow across the chest, pull my purple running shoes on, and just go, out the door and away, my body emptied of anything but movement through air and what that movement makes of me. As predictable as the angle of light that summons it from wherever habit is stored in the book of the body, as exacting as the words I search for to describe it, running asks that I engage in a practice as difficult, disciplined, and liberating as the writing I do much of the rest of the time. Each day it requires that I inhabit my body as completely as possible, surrender to change, and let that process work on me until I am not the tired and often dispirited woman who leaves the house, but the one who returns enlivened, cheeks aflame, her mind swept clear as a Zen garden.

That's how it is on good days. On bad days I am not only indifferent to the summons, but resistant to the idea of even going out the door. It takes me half an hour just to get my running clothes on, and another half hour when, distracted by minutiae like clipping coupons, redoing my address book, or making a list of clothes I cannot afford from the latest Eddie Bauer catalog, I procrastinate to the point of absurdity, struggling to persuade myself even to stretch. An invisible force field holds me hostage from movement, and I fight the urge (not always successfully) to take a nap. Sometimes it's even dark by the time I finish all these negotiations with myself, and I am forced to scrap the whole deal on the basis of personal safety.

It's been this way for over twenty years, ever since I first started running in 1977. And though running, like writing, is something I've stuck to, one of the pages on which I have both discovered and written my life, I sometimes feel no more knowledgeable about it then when I first started, a two-pack-a-day, chain-smoking, writing-blocked graduate student who could barely make it around the block. The longer I run, the longer I practice (and I mean that in the meditative sense), the more mysterious the process becomes. Not just exercise, but a way to get in touch with and reclaim myself in an often fragmenting world, running also serves as a powerful antidote to clinical depression, a metaphor for the creative process, and, in its most profound moments, a spiritual practice.

I grew up in rural Pennsylvania and New York State, where I hiked around the woods daily and regularly walked or bicycled long distances to my friends' houses. But around age eleven, I began to avoid sports, considering myself "unathletic," a clod, someone who couldn't do it. Later on, in high school, I envied the trim, popular cheerleaders like Allyson Buzzini and Alexandra Von Kuhn as they did cartwheels along the sidelines, somehow managing, in their mini-skirted blue and gold corduroy uniforms, chests emblazoned with an NS for North Salem, to combine sexiness with sports. And I feared (and, I must confess, looked down on) broad-shouldered, mannish girls like Beth Algae who thundered down the polished gym floor during girls' games, dribbling the ball as fast and skillfully as any boy. I knew Beth could pound me.

Deep in my bones, I believed all these girls possessed skills of which *I* would never be capable. Somewhere along the way I had misplaced, relinquished, or buried any sense of myself as an adept or able female body, let alone as a distance runner. But then, *no* girls I knew really ran for the sake of running itself. There was no girls' cross-country team at NSHS in the '60s and early '70s. And track season, for girls, consisted of the fifty- and hundred-yard dashes and a feeble exercise that measured how many feet we could throw a softball. I ran the ludicrous distance, feeling diminished by it before I even began.

How did this come to be? When I look for models of active women I find only unfinished portraits, partial trails, incomplete instructions. My mother was an accomplished tennis player, horse-woman, and skier. She died when I was nine. Her pewter tennis trophies gleamed in a back pantry cupboard for years, mysterious as small grails. And her cowboy boots (from her summer working on a dude ranch in Wyoming) ended up in our dress-up box. In one of my favorite photographs, she stands poised, in the clunky skis of the '40s, before a precipitous chute on Mount Snow. Even my step-mother, a depressive who sometimes barely stirred from her bed, had been an excellent swimmer when she was young. Different as they were, both women seemed to have put that part of themselves away to become mothers of the '50s, with all the restrictions on the female body that era implied. Mothers definitely didn't run.

Had the mothers ever been girls? Had they ever been anything other than mothers? Had they ever felt the urge to move, the way she did, faster and faster, legs spinning like a broken second hand. It is not something she even thinks about, moving this way, the times when her cells suddenly throb and leap, when she is so full of energy she can't not run *but moves, insistent, swallowing the air like milk, sucking in great cool gulps of it despite cries of "Stop running," or "No running here." There is salt on her lip. She is a car. She is a thunderstorm. She is the world itself, and the sound it makes turning on its invisible axis as she runs and runs, all verb, all movement, all pulse.*

Mothers didn't run. But I did. When I recall my early childhood, I am always outside, a blur of motion as I chase a red kickball or play Fox and Geese on long summer evenings. I still remember the afternoon at Wyndcroft School, when I "got" the hang of hoop racing, running along behind the steel ring, its handle warm in my hand, everything perfectly balanced. On Field Day that year I got a blue ribbon in the third-grade hoop race and a red ribbon in the running relay. And there was a time, between about the ages of seven and nine, when I believed I was really a girlhorse. A shiny black filly with ripple to her gallop, wearing a tuxedo blaze and two pairs of white stockings, who galloped up and down our road for hours. When a real horse, Chestnut Hill, broke for the river one hot afternoon during my lessons, I clung to his back, too excited to be scared, aware only of myself as an extension of his powerful, surging body. It was a feeling I would not recapture for years until it returned me, one hot afternoon, running on fire roads in the San Gabriel Mountains, and I was both horse and rider again, moving together in one smooth purl of motion.

I lost touch with that part of myself for many years. If, as poet Stanley Kunitz has said, "our best songs are body songs," I not only put mine away, I didn't even know such songs—or what they celebrate—existed. Looking back, I catch only an isolated glimpse of one here and there. I see myself playing left wing in field hockey, bright blue pinney coming undone, braids flying as I dash up and down the side of the field, loving the position because it lets me run. I see myself walk-jogging four miles to Lake Mamanasco just to suntan myself for a couple of hours. I see myself in a pack with my siblings, making a ritual run down Hunt Mountain each night the summer my stepbrother tried to commit suicide and my parents' marriage began to break up. I hike the woods in North Salem or at Bish-Bash Falls with my boyfriend, cutting cross-country when we get bored with the trail. I climb the mile-long hill behind our house to the area we kids called the pine forest to camp out summer nights in high school. There is movement everywhere.

But what I remember most is watching boys run. I've always been attracted to runners, beginning in ninth grade, when my first boyfriend, Lee Richardson, ran cross-country; and I dated several other runners during high school. Whenever I could summon the courage, I went to home meets, which always seemed to occur in a body-numbing, bone-chilling November rain. I'd stand, umbrella-less, my maroon pseudo-benchwarmer growing progressively more drenched and heavy, just to catch a glimpse of my heartthrob as he placed himself at the starting line, his number (which I got to keep afterward, if he remembered) fluttering in the wind. Coach Osborne muttered something inaudible about the course, raised his starting gun, shot it, and they ran, like a pack of hounds, across the soccer field and into the woods.

The race really happened in the woods. We didn't see the boys again till near the end of the race when they emerged from the bare, black trees in a ragged line, sprinting for the finish. By this point, the runners' bodies would be flushed with cold beneath their skimpy blue and gold singlets. The muscles and veins in their legs stood out like those on marble statues. Their skin was splashed with mud. They looked like racehorses, chests heaving, flecks of foam around their mouths, and sometimes, after they'd crossed the finish line, they'd double over with dry heaves while Coach threw a blanket over their shoulders and thumped their backs, shouting, "Way to go, Richardson." It seemed a heroic and completely male world, not one where I had any place.

Then it was over. I'd come for my glimpse and that was it. The guys jogged back to the one-story, redbrick school for hot showers and locker room horseplay. My face numb, my hands chapped and freezing, the last school bus long since gone, I turned for home, half walking, half running the two and a half miles along Route 124 before I came to our road. Sometimes I stopped partway home to warm up in Thompkins' store before returning to my steady dogtrot. It never even occurred to me that, while I may not have been running over hill and dale the way the cross-country runners were, I was doing exactly what they did, over about the same distance.

She runs, though she would not call it that, does not even think to describe it as anything other than a way to stay warm and get home more quickly. A way to both quell and flee from the anxiety of watching whatever boy she is love with that season. She runs, racing herself and the accordion-wheeze of her chest, the push-up squeeze of her heart, the flip-flop, slam feet both toward and away from something. She runs, and it disappears. In the needling rain-that-is-almost-snow, she slips and slides, putting one foot before the other and back again, automatically, unthinkingly, the body, the faithful, recalcitrant body pushed to do its job and responding. Each inhale opens like a paper flower in water. Each exhale explodes like a shower of fireworks. The two together are a deep swig of air. She runs through air and is momentarily airborne, no longer a girl on edge, watching from the sideline, but one of the runners herself, slicing seconds from time she will not even remember.

The only time I ever approached running with anything resembling intention was during my senior year in high school. For about a month that spring, I rose earlier than anyone else in the house, threw on a pair of cutoff jeans and a purple tie-dyed shirt, and laced myself into my red Converse high-tops. I took off down the thickly wooded corridor, my feet slapping the oiled dirt of Fields Lane in the rhythm of a four-beat line. I ran for at least a mile before I turned and came back, huffing and puffing but curiously elated. I knew nothing about running. I didn't know to stretch beforehand, or how to pace myself, or even how important it is to have the right shoes. I just, as the Nike ads were to say fifteen years later, did it.

She runs. Every morning she wakes up with something pulling at her, something that draws her from bed to the road, entranced. She does not know why she goes or what it is except that she must run, flinging her body down the tunnel of trees, the green throat that swallows her until she is nothing but breath. It is all she knows to do this last spring at home. It is how she gets ready to go, leaving and returning in this way, practicing how it feels to move with nothing other than her own strong legs. She does not even think of it as running. Does not even think of it as anything at all but this thing she does, going away from home and coming back again, nothing different, but everything changed, as if she is practicing for something, the fast flutter of heart, the wingbeats of breath, the surge of her quadriceps all she needs, as if moving this way will freeze it all, her parents' white farmhouse stopped in time like a painting. Untouched. And she the only thing moving, slender figure of a girl in the landscape, who moves to keep it whole.

And then, just as inexplicably, I stopped. I remember my father telling me that he thought what I was doing was plain crazy. What was I trying to prove anyway? Maybe he was worried that I would somehow hurt or injure myself with this sudden passion. Or perhaps he didn't want me out there alone so early in the morning. I no longer remember his exact words, only that they had a completely deflating effect. They weren't, I think, the reason why I stopped running. But they certainly didn't support me in the process. Yet something of that young woman remained alive in me, like a flame turned down low on a gas stove. When I began running seriously five years later, it flared right up, as if it had always been there, like a conversation between good friends for whom time and distance make no difference.

II.

I started running for real when I met my first husband, David, at graduate school in California. A distance runner long before marathons became a craze, David was, and remains, the most devoted practitioner of the sport I've ever known. Running was David's passion, bliss, and obsession. He took it as seriously as I was beginning to take writing, though with considerably less resistance to the process. He courted me through both the haze of my cigarette smoke and my scoffing and disbelief that he actually covered the distances he did. "Are you making that up?" I'd ask, aghast, when he mentioned, over what had become our daily afternoon tea, that he'd put in a twenty-mile training run that morning. "No," he said, grinning, obviously pleased at my shock. I was hooked.

Oddly, though, I can't remember the first time I ran again. I know I practiced running through a wooded area called the Wash at Pomona College while studying for my master's exams. David had gone to Hawaii for two weeks and I resolved to begin while he was gone. I walked down there each day with my Filipino roommate, Lisa, who insisted on going along for my safety. Wearing the same red sneakers I had in high school, still not aware of the importance of stretching, I set out, circling the two-mile loop through the live oaks as if I knew what I was doing. And on some level, I did. Despite smoking and inexperience, I ran two miles straight off.

But I started for earnest that summer. By then David had taken me to get real running shoes. This was before they made women's shoes; I had to make do with a pair of men's red Nikes, which now seem as insubstantial as racing flats. With David's gentle and patient coaching, I began with laps around our block in Pomona, gradually working up to laps around tree-shaded Lincoln Park a mile up the street. Though I have one memory of successfully completing a requisite number of laps around the block and realizing I really could do it, there is no clear dividing line. There was a time before running and a time after it, when it seemed like I had always been doing it.

Running moved me into the landscape. In fact, so much of my becoming a runner is tied up with having done so in southern California that it's hard for me to separate the activity from the locale in which it was first practiced. When I think about my first years of running, I see myself always against the backdrop of the San Gabriel Mountains, a small figure in a landscape of massive granite folds that is itself still emerging, still in the process of change. I see the sprawling gray dome of Mount Baldy, the ten-thousand-foot peak visible from everywhere in the valley. I see myself on the fire roads above Claremont, a bevy of California quail scattering at my approach like a group of excited abbots, their distinctive, black crown plumes bobbing as they burble among themselves.

I see myself that first summer, when we were house-sitting for friends in Mount Baldy Village, on the Glendora Ridge Road, my lungs stinging with altitude as five black-tailed deer bounded across the road before me. Back home in Pomona, I ran, nearly daily, at Puddingstone, the local, then still quite primitive regional park where seven coyotes crossed my path one morning and I once saw a rare black-footed ferret. I see myself running at the beach, salt spray mixing with my own sweat. And of course I see myself in my own neighborhood. I see myself in my own neighborhood, loving every bungalow and pink stucco cottage, every palm, orange tree, olean-der, and bougainvillea. I see myself wrestle with heat, getting up at 5 A.M. to run on summer days when the temperature climbs to a hundred degrees. I see California and the way running led me into it, later hiking and cross-country skiing, by giving me a kind of confidence in my body I hadn't had before.

She runs and becomes the air itself, blowing down the side of the mountain. She runs and the landscape comes inside her body, bay laurel and sage burning in her lungs. She cannot tell where the scent leaves off and she begins, canyon heat beating a tattoo in her head, cismontane. Her legs seem to move by themselves and she is *the black-tailed deer, the mountain lion, the coyote that once runs beside the road for a mile, his gaze green and wild as the foothills in the brief California spring. She runs. Through manzanita, silk-tassel bushes, western mountain mahogany, she runs, at home in her body for the first time in her life. Sometimes she picks rock roses and carries them home, the pink, fire-resistant petals falling from her hands as she moves.*

I ran. But when I search for who my models might have been during those early years of serious running, the screen of memory again comes up blank. I was aware, of course, of champion women runners, people like L.A.'s own Mickie Gorman, reigning distance queen Greta Waitz, and later Joan Benoit. But they were the elite, people I read about in *Runner's World,* or *Track and Field News,* not bumbling beginners like myself, who sometimes had difficulty making it out the door and for whom the goal of three miles a day, every day, was a hard-to-realize dream. The only other woman runner I even knew was Birthe Neibecker, the Danish wife of David's best friend. But she lived in San Gabriel, a half hour away, so we rarely ran together, except in races where, anxious and dry-mouthed, each afraid we'd do something "wrong," we'd struggle to balance camaraderie and competition. From the beginning, running was something I did alone, a silent way of companioning myself that never felt lonely.

Which perhaps accounts for my brief career as a racer. With David as my coach, it was inevitable that I tried racing. Though he never pressured me to do so, watching him race made me curious. I also wanted to enter more completely into this world that was so important to him in the way he was learning to enter into my writing. Though I was not then and have never been fast (running under eight-minute miles my only goal), before I knew it I was racing. A 5K at the Azusa Golden Days that first fall was followed by a Bonne Bell 10K for women, countless other 10Ks, and finally, in 1978, a half marathon at Mission Bay in San Diego. But the half marathon marked some kind of turning point for me. I had proved to myself that I could go the distance. Riding home in our '66 Volkswagen Bug, chilled and shaky, my intestines writhing, I was both exhilarated and exhausted.

She runs. Farther than she ever has in her life. She runs as if she will never stop running, as if the race will never end, as if she will be doing this forever, the race one long ribbon of energy she becomes, the rhythm of her own breath moving her forward like a musical note, like a sandpiper, like a muscle become air and light. She runs, legs lifting until she thinks she cannot lift them anymore, arms pumping, her body dissolving around her until she is nothing but breath moving against itself like the raspy tongue of a cat. Until she has done it, the last miles excruciating, the finish line like the vanishing point on a horizon she will never reach but then does, flecks of saliva like dried seafoam around her mouth. She doubles over, then stands again, her legs hardly knowing what it means to stop. Then stopping. It is over. She has done it, and in the doing taken the running so far inside herself it is as if she has engraved her cells with movement, each molecule, each spiral of DNA encoded with the ability to cover the distance that has been with her since the beginning of time.

Running had been an important way of claiming my identity. But in order to make it fully my own, I had to do away with the trappings as they had come to me from David. I stopped racing. Though my times had improved with each race, it was always an excruciating experience for me, one that, I realized, detracted from the pleasure of running. I was used to running alone, where my times didn't matter to anyone but me. I enjoyed running as much for the opportunity to look around as for the workout it gave me. A private activity that began to assume dimensions akin to meditation, running restored me to myself after a day at work and afforded me a space in which to think about my writing. I felt anxious and overexposed in a crowd, scrutinized by both other runners and observers in a way that made me feel bumbling, inadequate and ugly, no matter how hard I'd trained.

The half marathon also helped me realize that I didn't want to compete. Somehow, over time, without my quite realizing it (and even as I dutifully recorded my distances and times), running had become something else, a spiritual practice, a form of what runner-writer George Sheehan might call *being,* sometimes more closely related to certain states I associated with writing than anything else I did in my life. I didn't run for the competition; I ran for how it made me feel, for the clarity and authenticity of the body at work.

III.

The decision to stop racing and to eventually stop even timing my runs was liberating, though at first I felt like a failure. But as time went on, I knew I had made the right decision. With the pressure off, running became something different, a process I could learn from rather than pit myself against. It empowered me in more ways than I probably realized, giving me both confidence in my ability to do things and the fitness to do them. There have even been several junctures when running came close to saving my life, proving itself to be braided into my being at such a deep level that I refer to it automatically in times of stress, danger, and loss. Though my first impulse at such times may be to quit, there is in me a deeper, bodily knowledge that knows running is not just a metaphor. To stop running is, for me, to symbolically stop breathing. To stop breathing is to say no to life, to myself, to the sense of being vitally present on the planet.

The first time running helped me save myself was in 1986 when I suffered from and was eventually hospitalized for an episode of clinical depression. I actually stopped running then for over a month. With my anxiety level so high I was nearly psychotic and my brain chemistry misfiring, running seemed to exacerbate the situation, triggering panic attacks each time I went out (though as in the past, I always felt better afterward). It was one of the few times in my life when will alone was useless. Even if I had wanted to, I simply could not *make* myself run. I couldn't make myself do *anything,* whether it was writing, sleeping, or eating.

I knew, even while hospitalized, that to relinquish exercise was to relinquish part of myself. And so I began to work out each day on a dusty old exercise bike that was in the community room of the Open Unit. Over the course of a week or so I built my stamina back up enough that I was soon out on an hour's pass each evening, walking briskly, then beginning to jog slowly around the residential neighborhood that surrounded the hospital in Upland. At times it felt like moving through hip-deep mud, or concrete that had already begun to set, but I kept going. I forced myself to continue, using my own breath as lifeline back to the ordinary world. Gradually the sense of enforced effort fell away and I was, if not well, then

at least more myself again, my mind clearer, my anxiety slowly dis-
pelled. I still remember the moment when, looking deep into the
recesses of a live oak as I cooled down, I realized I had been
returned to the world.

When I got out of the hospital I worked myself slowly back up to
a mile, then two miles, and finally, on good days, three miles a day,
running down the country road where we had moved in western
Oregon. Though my resolve wavered and I wanted to stop with
every step, I chanted to myself, in a voice I thought of as my dead
mother's, *You can do it; you can do it. Good girl; you're almost home.
Home, home, home. The body is home.*

*She runs. She runs and she returns to herself, sees her own face and
the land around her come back into focus as she heads out through the
sharp, resinous scent of Douglas fir and ocean mist that cascades over
the Coast Range, Mary's Peak floating before her like a great gray
whale. She runs, and bit by bit light breaks through the clouds the way
it does in March, streamers of clarity opening within with each breath,
the way the sky does above her. She runs, down Priest Road, then out
onto Route 20, where the loggers begin to recognize her and honk
encouragement as they barrel past. She runs, the showers that come and
go blending with her sweat, soaking into her T-shirt until she cannot
tell where she begins and the rain leaves off. She runs, no divisions
between herself and the movement, and in the running returns. There is
sweat on her lip and trickling down her neck. When she goes up Wren
Hill her lungs burn. Her legs ache. But she keeps running.*

The running carries her home. Carries her to the moment when, all breath, all pulse, she finishes and walks through her backyard, seven acres of meadow and riverfront. She walks and breathes, her skin alive to the small silver hands of the rain that touch her everywhere, cool, gentle, alive, that say to look up. She looks up and sees the fog break over the peak at the same moment it clears in her head. The fog breaks and her mind is a mirror again, clear, focused, exact. She sees herself, a woman in her early thirties with tangled brown hair who falls down on knees in the garden amid primroses and mud, giving thanks for each breath that has brought her to this moment of return and self-possession.

The second time I fell back on running was when I went through a divorce. Afraid of losing everything, from the roof over my head to my shaky sense of self in the wake of David's departure, I forced myself to keep running. I used running not as an escape from the horror of the whole experience but as a way to work through it. Though it made me sad and lonely at times (particularly because it was so bound up in my mind with David as runner), my runs during the separation and divorce taught me that running really was my own. Motivated at times by anger ("I hope you keep running," David had said when he left, as if taking credit himself for what I did), at times by despair, I ran toward someone in myself, the shape of who I might be, even as I invented her. I called her Running Woman and knew only that she was fleet-footed and elusive, like the deer I've always identified with without knowing why. Running permitted me to gather the broken shards of myself together, melt them down, and pour them back into the container of who I was again.

She runs, sometimes weeping as she moves, the fierce tooth of winter in Wisconsin biting into her bones, gnawing all the way through the contracted fist of her heart that beats on, faithful, unfailing. The frozen lake beside her is like tundra, the road ahead a path that appears and disappears beneath ghost-tracks of snow. The wind cuts through her polar fleece mask. Thirty-below-zero wind chill. If she stops she could die, like all those stories she read in childhood about falling asleep in the snow. But she does not stop. She continues. She follows the breath that becomes the road that becomes the heat of her own cells warming her body, fire at the center of the rose. She runs and the petals open inside her, print themselves on her tissues, and then in the air where her breath hangs in small clouds that take a long time to vanish. Her back steams through three layers of clothing. She runs and runs and runs. Runs until she is no longer cold, no longer frightened, no longer alone but a friend again to herself, a woman running who remembers the girl from so long ago, the girl who needed only movement and her own good legs. She is her own good legs, and they carry her.

Alison Townsend is a poet, essayist, and reviewer whose writing has appeared in many magazines, including Calyx, Prairie Schooner, The Georgia Review, *and* The Women's Review of Books. *Her work has been anthologized in a number of collections, most recently in* Claiming the Spirit Within: A Sourcebook of Women's Poetry *(Beacon) and* Dying: A Book of Comfort *(Doubleday). She teaches English and creative writing at the University of Wisconsin–Whitewater, as well as In Our Own Voices, a private writing workshop for women.*

Kate Kinsey

The Breath of Weightlessness

Howler's Meadow got its name from the screech owls that wailed it up to the moon and stars. No one walked there after dark because of the feathery ghosts that swooped soundlessly and sometimes released otherworldly cries that mingled with their prey's terrified squeaks. Well, at least no one we knew walked there after dark. We dared each other enough times but when mothers called "Dinnertime!" we scattered obediently. The truth was apparent to all the neighborhood kids—it was a killing field, filled with vengeful spirits.

During the daytime we learned to fly there. Howler's Meadow had a straight stretch between the oaks and evergreens leading to a ridge that looked like the single stone entrance to the fairy's underground world. From that lookout, we saw everything from magic kingdoms to pyramids to Gotham City. The drop was about fifteen feet down and twenty feet across, enough to convince us we were heroes, and more than enough to agonize our mothers. Miraculously, no one ever fell. We would start at the back of the meadow and run hell-bent to the ledge, stopping precariously close to our demise in order to embrace the wind hugging us back across our chests and under our outstretched arms. That was flying and I was immortal at that moment. I was Wonder Woman and Underdog, Isis and every one of those fearsome ghosts for one perfect instant, before my feet shuffled to keep my balance and I fell flat into suburban childhood again.

I've never given up the belief that I am meant to fly. Not with the metal planes and toys that the boys invented, but naked, myself, just reaching out to the clouds, the wind sweeping across my belly and streaming my hair back. I know I am meant to see the rolling fields and the soft-textured trees from up above, where I can take it in whole, but still in pieces, because I am not God yet. My wings are new and wet, so I run, ready for the breath of weightlessness.

For the longest time, I was my kite. It was made in the face of an Oriental man, his mustaches the long, black tails of it. I would run, his chin bobbing against the ground until he rose, gracefully unrolling into the sky and smiling down at the little girl who still ran, trying futilely to trade places. As soon as I read *Peter Pan* I knew that somewhere in London another little girl had succeeded. The magic truly began when I saw Mary Martin play the little boy with the fairy dust that helped wishes fly. It finally made sense then. It was women who became boys who were the magic ones, who loved and kissed the girls in nightgowns and held their hands as they flew to Never-Never-Land.

I never told anyone about running and flying, how they were wound about like snakes slithering through my body. I never told because I knew someday I wouldn't be allowed to do either. Fundamentalist households have an invisible time when girls become ladies and ladies don't run, they don't shout, and they will never, ever fly until Jesus calls them home. That day came in first grade when I was told to put my shirt back on and get in the house, now. For the next twelve years I lived in a lovely cage. It had a relevant mix of piety and designer labels, including incest and anorexia. When they released me, it was nine years before I ran again. By that time, my body was locked into the proper submissive posture: legs pressed together so nothing fertile could flow, hips drawn tight and uninviting, head bowed to the God in whose image I was not made, eyes lowered so I could see only the dirt that once sprang up to meet my feet. I was frozen so deeply, I could barely get my fingertips past my knees, and could run no more than the length of the driveway. But my soul remembered what my body could not and I began to dream of flying again.

Mornings were best because people were intent on clasping those last, most precious moments of sleep. In the cool stillness, I allowed awkward steps, sprinting the first quarter of the block and then walking, panting, counting the cement squares that led back to the safety of my downtown apartment. Every day at dawn, I put on my one pair of bulky sweats and "ran."

It was something to mention to coworkers who wanted to know how I stayed so skinny. Telling them the truth, that I'd starved myself for so long so I would never have those sweet feminine curves, was not an option. No one needed to know about flying. No one needed to know that becoming a woman would keep me banned from Never-Never-Land forever.

Flying soon followed. I learned how to fly on the swings in the vacant playground across the way. After a hard run through painful sidewalks on the Hispanic side of town, I would swing. Up, up, until the chain gave a little, saying I was as high as I could go, until my feet brushed the leaves of a forgotten oak, until the swoops moved the pain in my chest to my belly, until one more push would send me out and away from this desolation. That's when peace flashed her shadow across my face. That's when it didn't matter that my job barely covered rent and ten dollars a week for food, where it didn't matter that my phone never rang, there was no one to wake beside, there was no hope for a single woman to escape the poverty of her soul and body.

Running became the one event in my daily life that I looked forward to. Books and movies paled in comparison to the refuge of my feet slapping patiently in the fresh morning air. Then one morning it wasn't enough. I ran and swung with no release. Frantically, tears pouring down my face because I couldn't, just couldn't face the realness of my life, I ran the loop again. By this time, people could see me, so I couldn't go to the swing. Panic filled my throat, rhythmically punching my heart so hard my feet might well have never touched the cracked concrete. Collapsing in sobs and sweat on the orange carpet of my tiny tenement, I crawled, legs throbbing and cramping, to the telephone. I was already late for work and had lied too much, too often to tell the truth now, to say simply, "I just can't do it today. It hurts too much." Without dialing, I dropped the receiver back into its cradle, showered, broke every speed limit imaginable, and lied about my alarm clock.

Lying was a way of life. Lying about my food, lying about my body, my finances, my family. Knowing the truth of my life was too much to bear, so I hid it under words, hoping that they would come true just by being spoken. If I ran enough, and lied enough, maybe it would all disappear. Maybe my father would never have come to me when I was alone. Maybe I would never have gone with those enticing, dangerous women who became my lovers, maybe some-day someone would love me enough to tell me I was beautiful and good and smart and deserved to be happy. She would tell me this tenderly, firmly, and would not want anything from me except that I hear her. But God was watching from the beginning of my life, accurately noting every slip, every mistake into that celestial life ledger. It's hard work fooling God, keeping up His image of the perfect woman whom He damned from her creation. The morning I fell apart on the floor, I knew I had no hopes of His pearly-gated heaven and would have to make my own.

I wish I could tell you it was simple after that. I wish I could tell you the path was good, fruity dirt and my feet fell wide and easy on it, but it has been steel and sand, mud and plastic, full of traps and poison oak. The steps have been intricate and difficult, the trail rut-ted and prone to winding back on itself. Some days I cannot see the barest glimmer of sun for all the oozing, stagnant tangles I have to get through. It would not matter if I could make you a map of the treacherous land—it shifts its labyrinth for each new visitor and the only compass lies in your belly.

I don't go on the swings anymore, but I have learned more about flying. One day I fell in love with a magnolia tree and smelled her roots. Another day a friend and I went for coffee and talked so late into the night I saw stars on my way home. Still another time I kissed a woman on a hillside overlooking the ocean and felt the moistness seep through my clothes. Sometimes, now, I look in the mirror and like my body with its defined scars and muscles gained from persistence, nothing else. The trail hides and deceives, but there are spaces like Howler's Meadow where I can run. And there are moments when I fly, sweet mother, how I fly.

Kate Kinsey is a blissfully untortured writer. By day, she is a body-worker. She moonlights as an intern with ex–New York editor Cristina Salat. She runs between fifteen and fifty miles a week on the beautiful Russian River.

Bettianne Shoney Sien

angels of nisene

the trees always recognize us
even if we don't recognize ourselves
lost in some great sorrow or exuberant love

flying

the golden leaves fall thickly
dancing on the path
rolling out a finely woven carpet
under our tender feet

a greeting fit for angels

rays of light stream
brilliantly down through the canopy
columns more majestic than any
man-made cathedral

catching our sweaty hair in a halo
for a second our arms become a brush of wings

whatever is said here
is as sacred as the rich brown winter creek roaring
or the whisper of redwood needles dropping
any tears shed
as important as the stark white frost painting the meadow
or dew caught like crystals in a spiderweb

we are each other's guardians
witnesses to the wonder of our strength
not immune to falling, or laughing with celestial mirth

brilliant as birds in our turquoise, scarlet, and plum
wise as coyote, muscular as mountain lions
sister to the deer
and the words we share
or don't have to say at all
echo throughout these enchanted woods
they are the poetry of our feet
chanting

this is who we are
this is who we are
this is who we are

Mary Hricko

Seasons of Change

I don't remember why I went out for track in high school, but there I was, the type of athlete who was indifferent about everyone and everything. I was scouted as a strategic distance runner with great strength and speed, but deemed unreliable and inconsistent. Sure, I was capable of running the better times, but I would run as fast as necessary to win the race, even if that meant running well below my potential.

My careless attitude infuriated my coach, who felt I was wasting my ability. In response to what she considered my substandard performances, she would make me run laps over and over again until I understood what I had done wrong. I'd run around that gray graveled track for miles and miles, but it never got me anywhere. It only made me more stubborn, I suppose.

Even my father who knew me best would watch from the bleachers and tell me that I should put more heart into my races. He scolded me for sitting on my talent and told me I would never be a true champion until I cared about what I was doing. He preached on and on about dedication and discipline, but was forever met with my indifference. Almost every chance I could, I told him not to come to my meets. I told him he made me nervous and that I didn't want him there. Yet no matter what I said or how mean I had said it, I could always find him in the stands, in his favorite maroon jacket, waving at me.

He'd stand tall, high above the crowd as if he were a giant watching over everyone. I would see his lean figure still and alert, not wanting to miss one movement of my pace, using his wrist-watch to time my splits. Now and then, he'd cup his left hand and scribble down the results of each split on the back of a paper he kept in his wallet. Years later, I found that paper among his things. At that moment, I realized how important it was to me that he was there, but as an arrogant and self-centered seventeen-year-old, I would never admit this.

In September 1992, my father died unexpectedly. He fell asleep in his chair one night and never woke up. In my grief, I withdrew, remaining distant from my friends and brooding to my family. Those close to me sensed the change in my demeanor and tried to bring me back to the person I had been, but I resisted every inter-vention.

Life without my father made everything seem still. My heart was broken, numbed by the shock of his death. I could hardly feel any-thing at all and concluded that this was the way life would always be. Feeling nothing, ever again.

I somehow managed to go through the motions of living. I redi-rected my focus on teaching, went to school and then went home. That was the routine I had mastered. The only comfort I allowed myself was a run around the high school track. I'd go there in the after-school silence and run quietly, thinking of all the things I wanted to run away from. It was a moment of escape, a place where I could control everything—the distance I ran, how fast I would run, and where I was going.

Sometimes I would run so hard, I made myself vomit. I don't know why I ran like this, maybe it was my way of dealing with my grief. I had to purge myself of it. Maybe I thought this was the only way to do it.

One night I ran fifty-seven laps around the last lane of the track because I was upset about something. Finally, a friend, who was the high school track coach, called out from the stands for me to stop. We had known each other for some time, competing against each other as athletes, working together as colleagues. We often ran together after her team's practices and talked about work and general things.

On this particular night, she told me that she'd never seen anyone run so much and that I ought to redirect my energies into something more productive. I mused over her observation, but said little. She promised me that she would find me something to do, but I paid little attention since it was the end of their season and she was moving to Indiana.

Weeks after she had left, I received a note in my mailbox that the school principal wanted to see me. I couldn't imagine why, but soon realized that I had been the victim of a conspiracy.

"Wendy told me you wanted to coach track next year." Before I could even protest, I was being thanked for taking on the responsibility. "I know you'll do a good job," the principal smiled. "I see you running round the track all the time." I left the office dumb-founded.

Track. Coaching. Me. The three words sifted through my thoughts. I didn't want to coach track. I considered turning around and telling the principal that a mistake had been made, but some unknown force would not allow me. I couldn't explain it for anything. I just kept on walking down the hall.

Although I had conceded, the more I thought about what I had agreed to do, the more I regretted it. I knew the team I was inheriting. I had watched them lose every meet the season before. They were a whiny bunch, more worried about their social skills than their athletic abilities. They didn't like to get dirty or sweat or run. They were a bunch of babies, complaining all the time that practice was too hard or too long. This was the track team I would be coaching unless I did something to change their attitude.

I began my assignment by seeking out the assistance of the one of the school's gym teachers, who gave me a good idea of which girls were athletically inclined. More important, he gave me copies of their agility tests. By the end of the week, I knew who could run, who could jump, and who could throw a softball over 120 feet. After recruiting between each class-period change in the lunchrooms and the hallways, I held a brief team meeting after school one day and told the group that open gym practice would begin on Valentine's Day.

"Be there if you want to be on the team," I said.

Almost immediately, the girls realized that our practices would not be sugar-coated. We spent the first week running up and down the steps for an hour at a time, sprinting in the halls, and doing agility drills over and over again in the gym. The next two weeks were spent out in the snow. I cleared the first two lanes with a borrowed shovel and had the girls run their workouts in the bitter cold. They hated me for it because it was hard.

One day when it was thirty-four degrees, the bravest of the bunch spoke up, complaining that I was cruel and heartless to make them run outside while the boys' team practiced in the gym. I responded by telling them I didn't have time for crybabies, and if they didn't feel like doing what had to be done, they could just go home. I turned around and went back to the track and started running. As I ran, I figured I'd be left alone—but as I looked over my shoulder I could see, one by one, the girls pushing themselves through the sludge behind me.

Our season began on a twenty-eight-degree day with four inches of snow and raining sleet. Everyone had hoped the officials would call the meet, but it went on as scheduled, and while the boys' team shivered and shook, cowering under their blankets, I watched my girls run around the track, warming up for their races, undaunted. Then and there, some of them realized why we had trained the way we did. Even though no one really talked about it, it marked the beginning of their trust in me, the beginning of our confidence in each other.

Although our team put forth a good effort, we lost our first meet by two points. The girls' 4x100 relay team blamed themselves because they were disqualified for having passed the baton out of the exchange zone. They had won their race by twenty meters but the celebration of their victory was silenced by the second zone judge, who waved the red disqualification flag. I didn't want to believe my girls had made the mistake, and even questioned the official's call, since the judge was associated with the team that had placed second. I soon learned that you cannot argue with officials. One of the girls who had made the "bad" exchange began to cry. I told them all to just forget it, that one race did not make a career, that it didn't matter what had happened. We knew who won the race that day, and I promised them they'd get another chance to prove it.

The rest of our season, we did fairly well. The team began to run with greater confidence. I assured them of their ability and reminded them that no matter how much talent they believed their opponents possessed, it was the effort they put forth and the attitude they maintained that would determine the outcome. This theory was proven time and time again and helped foster strength within the girls.

Many were able to overcome their fears of competition. Such was the case of one of my favorite athletes. She had been having some trouble with her knee; the pain had forced her to pull out of a relay during two of our meets. At our next meet, a big invitational, I decided to scratch her from her individual races so she could reserve her strength for the relay. She was a reliable handoff, and it was easier to replace her in the individual events.

Soon after my decision, the father of our anchor runner came to me. He went on and on about how this particular girl had caused the relay team to lose their event the week before and how I was foolish to let such a poor runner race.

"You're a bad coach! You don't know what you're doing! How stupid are you?" he yelled in the crowd, but I ignored him. The runner, who overheard his comments, came up to me and asked to be pulled from the race. She claimed she wasn't feeling well, but I knew that wasn't the case.

"I think you should put in someone faster," she told me. I stared at her face and could tell that she didn't want to forfeit her spot on the relay team. I asked her how her knee was.

"Okay, I guess," she said.

"Then you can run your race. I'm not taking you out of that relay." She looked at me, surprised, but went back to the others, who dared not challenge my decision. When I walked with them to check in with the officials, I pulled the runner aside and told her that she didn't need to listen to anyone but herself.

"You just go out there and run your race. You know you can."

I bit my lip as she grabbed the baton from her teammate and watched her run the fastest split of her team. Painful knee and all, somehow she managed to sprint those two hundred meters as if nothing was wrong. I felt pride burning in my face and ran over to her when she finished. It was important for me to look at her and nod. I then scanned the crowd for the father who had questioned my decision. I couldn't find him at first, but when I did, I glared into his eyes—what I had seen, what I had known. I said nothing to him at all. I didn't have to.

As the season continued, I taught my girls to be strong and find value in their performances even when they were running dead last. It was nice to win, but not all-important. I wanted them to like what they were doing. I wanted them to be different from the type of athlete I had been. I wanted them to care about each other—and they did.

It was important to me to run my team like a family. Everyone was responsible for everyone else, and to practice what I preached, I made certain to walk my athletes down to each official check-in and say something to each of them before their races. Then I positioned myself along the track where they could hear me call out to them. From there I would sprint as fast as I could to the finish line so they would see me waiting for them. I would hug them and then walk them back to the team, only to resume the ritual for the next event.

As the season went on, I came to feel for my athletes much the same way a parent feels for a child. And the more I became involved with my team, the more I began to regain the sense of myself I thought I had lost. In one way or another, that team, all forty-two of those girls, brought life back to me. They made me feel again. They made me find humor in the things I did.

There was the time I promised my 4x400 team that I'd kiss their feet if they set a new school record. It was one of our last meets of the season and they had come close many times. I felt that if ever a relay team deserved to set a new school record, it was these four girls. As we waited for the call of the race, I made them the promise and they laughed.

"No, I swear!" I said. "Toes and all."

The next day four girls stood on a bench, shoeless and sockless, as I stooped down before them and kissed each foot. The whole team stood around the victors and carried on with laughter. They knew I was a silly person, but they also knew I loved them best. Even today, members of that team still talk about the formal "foot-kissing" ceremony for the four girls—whose record has yet to be broken.

And there were even times when coaching went beyond the track. After a Friday practice, most of my athletes rushed to get home, but one of my hurdlers often lingered. She would help me put things away, but mainly she wanted to talk. When she was eight, her mother had abandoned their family. Now at fourteen she had so many questions about boys and everything else. It was awkward for her to talk to me about some things, but I guess she felt she could trust me. I took her under my wing because she was a really good kid.

Whenever I asked her to run a new event, I could always count on her to do it with no complaint. When all of our milers were out with colds and injuries, she volunteered to run the event so our team would have an entry in the race. I admired her determination. She was the type of athlete who would fall down, brush herself off, and start all over again.

One Friday, as we moved the hurdles from the track to the grass, she told me that the junior prom was coming up, and a senior had asked her. I teased her a little about the big event, but congratulated her all the same. She went on in a hesitant voice to tell me she had appreciated all I had done for her; I was the closest thing she had to a mother. She asked me if I could do just one more favor—could I go with her to find a dress. She explained that she didn't want to ask her father and, well, she figured she could trust me to help her. The following Saturday I, along with six members of my track team, spent a day at the mall trying on prom dresses, and later we saw a movie.

When we reached the most important meet of the season, the league meet, I marveled at the transformation of both the team and myself. The team I had not wanted to coach—Wendy's "Bad News Bears," as we had often referred to them—was now the team I had begun to love. The team that could possibly win a league championship. The practice before the meet, I sat with the girls on the track.

I began by telling them I was privileged to be with them. I explained to them how much it meant to me to be their coach. I told them about my father and my days as an athlete and thanked them for teaching me the things that I should have learned when I was their age.

The next day, as we sat in the bleachers, everyone held hands and we said our ritual team prayer. We showed each other our lucky charms. They'd brought all sorts of things, from pennies to jewelry to stuffed animals. I modeled my father's maroon jacket and old wristwatch. Together, we talked calmly about the meet. I told them that it was their day and to make the best of it. "You control the outcome," I said, "but have fun."

Even though we had done rather well much of the season, none of the other league teams expected us to be a threat. After all, we had lost all of our meets the season before and the defending league champion, Lakeview, was slated to win again. Furthermore, we had been given lousy lane positions, determined by our season's times.

The meet began with the hurdles. Both of my athletes landed in the lane against the fence, a lane I hated because there was always the risk a spectator would lean over and get in the way. The gun went off and the first heat began. My athlete led the way, but on the last hurdle, she clipped her spike on the fence and fell. She got up and placed second. It worried me because she was the stronger hurdler and I had hoped she would take first place.

My second hurdler must have read my mind because she looked at me with a smile: "Don't worry coach, I'll get it." The gun went off and as I watched, she ran through the hurdles with a vengeance, placing first overall in the event. We were off to a good start.

As the meet continued, we continued to do well. I said nothing because I didn't want my girls to get overconfident. We had several more events to go, including a crucial 4x100 relay. This was the rematch we had been waiting for all season—we'd be racing the team that beat us when we were disqualified. I told the four relay runners to leave the previous race behind them; this race belonged to us. We practiced handoffs as we waited for the call.

We walked down to the check-in and waited for our lane placements. We were right next to the team that won after our disqualification. The anchor of our team, a replica of myself at seventeen, looked square into the eyes of her opponent and said, " You better run fast." I had to turn away to hide my grin.

I returned to the other side of the track, where I could watch all the exchanges. I used my father's watch when the gun went off. My first runner rounded the curve and made a flawless exchange.

The second runner was being chased by her opponents, but she fought them off by bursting into a sprint along the straightaway. When she gave the baton to our third leg, the hand-off was perfect.

The third leg was our strongest runner. She ran her curve effortlessly and efficiently smacked the baton into the anchor's hand.

Our anchor took off as if we were trailing, but the truth was the other teams were nowhere near her. She continued to sprint at full intensity, and eventually I realized that she was running for the record.

I screamed and hollered and sprinted to the other side of the track, nearly colliding with people as I watched the seconds on the clock. I jumped up and down as I ran to the four girls, who were hugging each other in jubilation. Everyone felt the excitement. It was difficult to remain calm.

As the meet continued, we learned from the announcer that we were in second place. Parents came over and congratulated me for a second-place standing even though we had a few more events to run. I refused to accept that we would finish second, though. "It ain't over till the fat lady sings," I thought. No way. Not now.

Two freshmen were running in the 800 meters and I was worried their lack of experience would be a disadvantage, but we managed to take first and third. Seven more points to add to our score. The next race was the 200m, and our runners swept the event. Eleven more points. Everything was almost too good. I became incredibly nervous.

As the final event, the 4x400 relay, drew near, I calculated the scores once more: to win the meet, we had to win this last event. I said nothing as I hurried to gather my 4x400 group. I saw no purpose in putting pressure on anyone.

We walked down to the gate and went into our huddle. I told the girls to run the race as they always did, but remembering that it was the last race of the season.

"Make it special," I told them. "Not for me, but for yourselves." I bit my lip as they went to check-in. I felt like I was the one about to run.

While the officials spoke to them, I went around the track and told the rest of the team to line themselves all along the fence. I wanted them to cheer like they'd never cheered before. Everyone responded accordingly. I saw my athletes scattered along the track like maroon markers. I positioned myself at the three-hundred-meter mark as I so often did for my runners. The gun went off, and my heart was in my throat.

The first runner, by far the best 400 runner of the relay team, got off to a great start. The most graceful runner I ever coached, she ran like a gazelle, her form nearly flawless. I envied her stride and the way she made running seem so effortless. She held the league record for the 400 meters and I was happy she was on my team. I watched as she handed the baton to our power runner.

The second athlete, a real fireplug, ran pounding steps as if she was punching the track with each footstrike. I often worried that she would suffer from shin splints, but she was tough as nails and often amazed me at races with her strength and consistency. She ran well, but the second Lakeview runner came up from behind; at the halfway mark of their leg, they ran shoulder to shoulder.

The handoff was even, but our third runner had a slow takeoff. She began her race shadowing her opponent. One of the best relay athletes, she had already raced in the 4x200 and 4x100. I had wanted to rest her for the mile relay, but she wanted to run the 400. It was apparent how tired she was as I watched her face strain. I saw that she was crying and worried that she was in pain. I called out and asked if she was okay. She nodded. She was upset because she had given her opponent the lead. I realized then the girls knew they had to win this race.

I could see my athletes along the fence screaming and cheering excitedly. They knew what I knew. My eyes began to well with tears as I watched our third runner lurch forward to make her handoff. We were behind.

I swallowed the rock that was in my throat and climbed up on the fence to watch the final leg. The exchange was awkward and our last runner was a freshman. I worried that in her inexperience she would sprint to catch up. Stay back! Stay Back! I thought. I could hardly speak as I watched helplessly, hoping that she would run smart and not waste her energy. I concentrated hard and started talking out loud to myself.

"On her shoulder, baby! Stay on her shoulder!" I called out. I had wanted her to draft off the right shoulder of her opponent as they ran along the back stretch. I don't know if she heard me, but she did what I wanted. When they neared the 300-meter mark, I told my athlete to go. It was the place where I has so often practiced with my 400 athletes to begin their final sprint. One hundred meters to go. And off she went. It was as if she could read my mind, as if I was running beside her telling her how to run.

The other runner, baffled to see my runner taking off so early, ran to keep pace. The two girls ran within a stride of each other, side by side, one surging forward, then the other. At the top of the straightaway, I watched as some unseen force pushed my athlete two strides forward. We were in the lead. Soon two strides became three.

I jumped from the fence and sprinted to the other side of the track. It was a point where anything could happen. Races are won by less than a second, less than a lean, and so I screamed and screamed for my runner to sprint and sprint. "Faster! Faster! Now! Now!" I hollered.

I could see the members of my team all running toward the finish line screaming and jumping and screaming. People were jumping up and down in the bleachers. The noise was deafening. Parents from the crowd had pushed in front of me, and I had to climb over the fence to see the end of the race.

In the last ten meters, my runner pushed her way toward the finish line and won. Despite the attempts of the officials to keep everyone off the track, my girls poured onto the field, hugging each other. They were all screaming and cheering. I stood on the fence watching them. I was frozen there for a moment, staring at the clock and at the crowd. We had won the meet. We had won the league championship.

Soon they began to look for me. I heard them calling, "Coach! Coach!" I jumped down from the fence and ran over to the clustered 4x400 team, now smothered by their teammates. Soon I found myself in the middle of the group, my athletes all pulling and tugging at me.

I began to cry. I cried and cried as I looked up to the bleachers. "What's wrong coach?" one of my athletes asked. "Why are you crying?" But I didn't answer. Instead, I squinted at the lights high above the bleachers. For a brief moment, I swore I saw the ghost of a maroon-jacketed figure standing there waving his hand at me.

Mary Hricko was born in Youngstown, Ohio, to Andrew and Frances Hricko. She has four older brothers who may have (indirectly) contributed to her interest in running. After running track for several years, she became a teacher and coach of both cross-country and track, as well as working with individual athletes. Currently, she operates a coaching listserv titled XC-TRACK, which is designed to assist beginning coaches and athletes with information and discussion on issues related to track and field and cross-country. She is also the library director at Kent State University's Geauga Campus. She lives in Lordstown with her husband, Tom Pitko.

Roberta B. Jacobson

The Wolf Pack

I didn't get a chance to voice my opinion on whether or not I *wanted* to run. I'd joined the Women's Army Corps and when Aunt Sam yelled, "Double-time, march!" that's exactly what we all did—no matter if our feet were blistered and our lungs felt ready to pop. Army basic training was serious stuff. We'd run at 5 A.M. or directly after lunch or even at dusk—whatever they said, whenever they said.

As for myself, I'd never run in my life, save for a few laps around my high school gym in phys ed class. I was a true "tenderfoot." The first couple of days our platoon ran around an oval track, but soon we were running over steep hills, across sandy beaches, along winding forest paths. We would have run into the ocean had the drill sergeant pointed us in that direction, but luckily she never tried it.

Did we actually want to run? Well, as I said, nobody actually bothered to ask our opinion. At the outset, probably 98 percent of us would have opted *not* to run at the crack of dawn, but rather to stay in our bunks for a little more shut-eye. We complained, we griped, we cussed, "What, *another* run? Can't we ever just *walk* anywhere?" It wasn't as though we ever did anything when we got to our destination. We'd simply loop around and run back to where we'd started from.

By the third week of the torture, we had found a certain rhythm. We got in step and stayed in step, singing and clapping. The adventure of running somehow seemed easier. Whereas at the outset, a mile seemed a sheer impossibility, soon we were chalking up three or more miles in a single stretch and hardly complaining. Our attitudes had changed drastically. Hey, this wasn't so bad. Maybe it was even slightly enjoyable. We'd help drag along our almost-fallen comrades who were wiped out but too proud to stop.

No matter how exhausted we got, one thing was for sure, we never gave up. "I'm not going to quit if she doesn't. If they can do it, so can I." As distances increased, we became a pack of wild wolves, fifty females strong, charging along together, pushing ourselves to limits we'd never even imagined.

There was another, rather hidden, motivation to stay on our feet. When we weren't running, we were stuck in the barracks either scrubbing (a floor, a toilet, a hallway) or polishing (shoes, boots, anything metal). Running had distinct advantages.

We never ran indoors. No matter if we encountered sheets of rain, blinding sandstorms, or even late snow flurries, we'd be outside in the fresh air, left, right, left, so many hundreds of thousands of steps you couldn't keep count. Running had become our way of life.

As all things finally do, our eight weeks of training drew to a close. It was nearing time for fifty fast friends to part ways. Some would be shipped off to Korea, others to bases around the United States, many of us to Europe. The night before our graduation from basic training, we sat in a circle, our feet soaking in buckets of hot water, and laughed about how inept we'd been those first few days, how slow, how clumsy. It seemed a lifetime ago.

At our graduation ceremony, we marched around the parade field at a normal walking pace, but in our hearts we knew we were a wolf pack of strong women warriors—ready to run, run, run up against anything that dared to get in our way.

Roberta B. Jacobson is a forty-five-year-old American who has lived in Europe for over two decades. She has been published in Cats, McCall's, Women's Day, The Educated Traveler, Transitions Abroad, *and* Writer's Digest.

Cate Terwilliger

Marathon Woman: A Chance to Be Your Own Hero

I mailed the entry form for my first marathon after finishing a shorter race remarkable for its setting and drama: 13.1 miles of rural road and hilly forest trail under a high canopy of leaves.

Most of us were city runners resigned to noise, fumes, and congestion. Here, there were light footfalls and measured breaths, the heavy, sweet smell of impending rain, and the sight other runners gliding among trees like ghosts. A high rolling storm darkened the sky and cracked lightning over our heads, then drenched us as we ran the last two miles on open road.

Soaked and satisfied, I didn't realize then that running a marathon, twice the distance of the race I had just finished, did not mean simply twice the effort.

I had entered the Twin Cities Marathon, which starts in downtown Minneapolis and ends at the state capitol in St. Paul. The 26.2 miles in between, run amid splashes of October color along four lakes and the Mississippi River, have given the event a reputation as the most beautiful urban marathon in the country. More than 8,000 runners participate each year, supported by 4,000 volunteers and 200,000 spectators whose enthusiasm makes heroes of ordinary people for a few hours.

"It's kind of like the Ph.D. of public fitness accomplishment," says my friend Marcy, who has run multiple marathons, including Twin Cities. "There are very few times as an adult that you can go out and do something that's authentically difficult and be publicly lauded for it."

I had wanted to do a marathon 10 years earlier, when I was 24. The idea energized my running and helped tap the sense of emotional and physical well-being sports have always given me. But as I pushed training runs to 10 miles and then 12, the pleasure waned, replaced in equal measure by hard effort. Eventually, I let go of the marathon goal, and let soccer, softball, and cycling replace most of my running miles.

When I recently resumed running in earnest, I reconsidered. As an athlete, I felt my biological clock ticking. And at a time of personal and professional flux, I wanted one thing I could claim, a goal whose success or failure depended solely on me.

So I began to train, rarely running more than 40 miles a week—low for a marathoner—while gradually increasing the length of my twice-monthly long runs. I knew these runs were crucial to my success; I had to develop the physical and mental toughness to go the distance. So I ran 15 miles, 17, 19, and finally—two weeks before the marathon—21 miles.

During these runs, I was rewarded with a period of rhythmic, effortless motion, the kind of experience that makes runners go.

Then, somewhere beyond mile 13, they became work. Finally, they grew arduous and graceless as I struggled to finish. Then I popped a couple of ibuprofen and retired to a hot bath, resting my ice-packed knees and ankles above the water.

By the time I hobbled to the end of that 21-mile run—under a gray sky, against a biting wind—I was ready to abandon the marathon entirely. How could I possibly run the additional five miles required to complete the race? And what did it matter?

A week later, I ran 11 miles of hilly blacktop through the Minnesota North Woods, the last three in a cold, driving rain. But nothing touched me: I was warm and strong and, once again, sure.

There was nothing to do now but rest, eat pasta, and drink water until I could hold no more.

Olympic marathoner Frank Shorter says the marathon is only half over at the 20-mile point. Other experts describe two races, a 20-miler and a 10K. According to popular wisdom, runners hit the wall—a physiological stall as the body nears exhaustion—at about 20 miles.

Some runners say the wall is a myth; others hit it and crumple. In any case, the last leg of a marathon is hard work. "The minutes will feel elongated; the miles will seem stretched out in some evil way," writes runner Richard Benyo. "Your mind will be working against a body that seems to be working against itself."

Of the more than 6,200 runners who start the marathon with me, 5,100 finish. Some simply wear out, undone by too much exertion over too many miles. Others are broken by the hill just after mile 21.

Marcy had warned me about it. "You have this feeling like the earth has been devastated and we're the only people left," she had said. "And here we are plodding along, doing this stupid useless activity."

A few miles before the hill, as we crossed a high bridge over the Mississippi, I'd seen many runners slowing to a walk. Now their numbers increased until the avenue became a ragged river of the running and hobbling.

Throughout the race, we runners had been like Blanche DuBois in *A Streetcar Named Desire,* relying on the kindness of strangers. But now, as we plod farther, their cheers, the music, and even the narrowing gap between us and the finish line lose their power to propel.

My favorite spectator, a smiling cherub of a woman playing her accordion, continues to appear and reappear as if by magic. But even her winsome good cheer falls flat. Struggling between miles 22 and 23, head down, I am beyond encouragement. My knees feel like bags of rocks, grinding and grinding.

I am sputtering, about to stall, when I think of something Marcy told me about the taste of an orange late in the race. "It's better than food, better than love, better than sex," she had said. "It's like nothing in this world."

I gesture feebly to my friend Gretchen, who helped me train and is now riding along this last stretch on her bike, anxiously watching my slow progress. She hustles to a gap in the crowd lining the road.

"Or-ange," I wheeze.

"What?" Gretchen asks, drawing closer.

"Or-ange," I rasp, sounding like a cowboy begging for water under a Death Valley sun.

A half mile later, Gretchen reappears amid the spectators, extending one hand. Peeled orange sections decorate her flattened palm.

I grab one with greedy fingers and crush it between my teeth, dribbling juice down my chin. The orange is sweet and sticky and wonderful. At this moment it is better than love, better than sex, better than any other food I can imagine.

But it is not better than walking. So, just beyond mile 24, I fall back on a desperation technique recommended by Benyo: briskly pacing 100 steps, then running 500. The counting takes my mind off the disturbing, unfamiliar sensation that my knees are about to explode.

Near mile 25, the encouragement of another friend who runs alongside for several yards prods me back into a jog. Gulping water at an aid station, I glance at my watch and realize that the last few miles have not undone my chances of finishing in under four hours—my goal, assuming I finished at all.

The bells of the St. Paul Cathedral sound just up the road, and beyond that, the dome of the capitol gleams in the sun like a Holy Grail. I gather myself and run a strong last mile, past the green-domed cathedral, over the last rise and down the wide stretch of beautiful black road that ends with the finish line.

I punch the button on my watch as I pass beneath the banner, then slow my quivering legs to an awkward walk. I look at my watch: 3:59:54. A volunteer places a finisher's medallion around my neck. "Congratulations," she says, smiling.

This is what matters on the outside: The electricity of being among more than 6,000 runners clustered in the early morning chill, poised for the starting gun amid coffee-clutching well-wishers; the cheers along the course of people who catch your eye and call out the number pinned to your chest to speed you along, who ring sleigh bells and play instruments to distract you from your pain; the finish line, the medallion, the congratulations.

And this is what matters on the inside: The chance, during months of training, to know yourself in weakness and strength, and to persevere. As Benyo wrote, to confront your own lions, and be your own hero.

Cate Terwilliger is a longtime runner who tolerates asphalt but prefers the mountain trails of Colorado's Front Range. She is a staff writer for the Denver Post.

Suzanne Case

Redemption

On the last weekend in August, in search of a perfect summer and a good long run, my partner and I headed for the high country at Yosemite. Fortuitously we had snapped up some last-minute tent cabin cancellations at the High Sierra camps. Late Saturday morning we slid on our running shoes and sunscreen, grabbed our water bottles, and headed up the John Muir Trail along the Lyell Fork of the Tuolumne River. The alpine air was fresh, the sky cloudless, the vista stunning.

Tuolumne Meadows had always held a "center-of-the-universe" quality for me, which was surprising since I'd hardly spent any time there. This sensation had crystallized when I had scattered the ashes of a lover over Lyell Canyon by air many years back. She had been hit by a bread truck while crossing a street on her way to surprise me on my last day of law school. I was left to work through immense pain and a vast loneliness while I struggled to complete final exams, then the bar exam, then start a legal career. It was a powerful time called to mind by Paul Simon's words:

Losing love is like a window in your heart
Everybody sees you're blown apart
Everybody hears the wind blow

But it had also opened a window to a deeper spiritual life, a time full of meaning and connection that etched itself indelibly into my consciousness. I drew on this reserve more and more as the years passed, aware of a different way of seeing at all turns.

On this day Tuolumne Meadows recalled to me the redemption of love, as my partner Naomi, whom I had now been with for over a dozen immensely loving and growthful years, even married years, ran alongside me.

We crossed the footbridge over the Lyell Fork, a place of awe and grace, where smooth-flowing bodies of crystal clear water sidle silently between immense low sheets of granite lounging in green meadows, all guarded by snow-wrapped peaks in the distance. At the eighty-eight-hundred-foot elevation my breath soon came rapidly, despite the flat, easy trail, so I waved Naomi on. She had been far more passionate about exercise for far longer than I, and had the condition to show for it. As for me, I never responded to physical competition, internal or external, and preferred to run in the quiet of my own pace. We had agreed to go out for an hour, then turn around. I'd see her back at the beginning.

I was excited to have "discovered" this route for a long run. The trail wanders in and out of pine forest and open meadows, along the ever-present Lyell Fork. It goes out at least eight level miles with good footing before beginning to climb—a welcome change from the hills I usually ran in the Bay Area. The whole stretch lay in that magical zone just before timberline thins out the trees to rock and snow, where the air is pure and the scenery spectacular at every turn. As I followed the trail, I scoped out backpacking sites for next year's tenth annual niece and nephew camping trip, finding more than a few worthy of childhood memories. And having devoted my legal work to conservation, I found a particular satisfaction in that place.

For most of my life, I had run in short spurts, usually for a few weeks in the spring, then giving out as the weather turned hot. I used any excuse to temper my exercise regimen. Then, as I approached my thirty-ninth birthday, I surprised myself by beginning to run steadily, and longer. Six and a half miles became routine. One day I announced that I wanted to run a half marathon for my birthday. Triumphing on completing it at an Envirosports trail race in Big Sur, I decided, or was somehow driven, to go for the big one, the marathon. It was my own version of a midlife crisis, a challenge to myself to do the unimaginable. Amazed, even reluctant, Naomi agreed to train with me.

The weekend long run became, for a magical four months, the focal point for our week. I obsessed on running, to the exclusion of much of the rest of my life. I devoured books on conditioning. I monitored my heart rate ad nauseam. I flashed my quads in the mirror. I spent hours searching for the right trail or country road for our training distance of the week. Through this process we stumbled onto a formula for the perfect "day of rest," an experience that had completely eluded our work-engulfed, project-focused psyches to date. For our Saturdays became a medley of morning long run, sumptuous lunch with fine wine (and plenty of water to compensate for what we knew to be the error of our ways), and afternoon rest, our bodies too exhausted to do anything else, all the while endorphins heightening our awareness of beauty in life.

In March of that year I ran the Napa Valley Marathon, at a record-breaking snail's pace, immensely proud of myself. Proving, in my mother's words, "You can do anything you want—just not everything."

So on this day on the Lyell Fork it all came together—death, love, health, beauty, and nature. I blazed past day hikers; I enjoyed their impressed grunts at this woman who actually ran the trail. As the meadows opened up, Smetana's *Moldau* (which I had blasted on the car stereo while cruising through the park with the intention, now realized, that it play over in my mind as I ran) became the lively wanderings of the Tuolumne River through the sweeping landscape.

Then, to my rhythmic steps, I silently uttered the rhythmic words of what I could remember of the Kaddish, the ancient Aramaic prayer that Jews recite to honor the dead, yet which speaks not a word of death but only of the sanctity of life, the blessedness, the grace of life. Hallowed is life, transcending even the darkest moments of the soul. I spoke the affirmation for my lover from my former life, for a vibrant woman from work who had died unexpectedly several weeks before, for Naomi's aunt who had died of cancer several years before, for a friend who had died of AIDS the previous year.

Soon, it seemed, I approached my sixty-minute agreed limit. But I am obsessed with measurable distances (perhaps to prove my accomplishments to myself), so I continued on a bit longer until I reached some lakes that I recognized on my map. Finally I paused, luxuriating in a few stolen moments to catch my breath. I drank in a long draft of life-giving water, and briefly soaked in the sublime beauty of the place and the exquisite moment. Then I turned and headed back, awash with the blessings of life.

Suzanne Case, a conservation attorney, runs with her partner Naomi and dog Zeek in the Oakland hills. Some of her most inspired moments have come in unexpected flashes on trail runs, when Hawaiian songs, essays, and haiku pour forth from the abyss.

Harriet Susskind

Race for the Cure

One woman wears a flowered scarf
covering her bald head.
Her skin is wine dark.
She is wringing her hands
and her tears keep falling.

It is Sunday morning in Central Park.
Survivors, some ninety-plus among
three thousand and forty-one entrants
are running the races of their lives.
Don't cry, you want to say, but don't.

You are afraid to enter the panic.
They have all cried too much,
felt stings like Cleopatra's adder,
felt shame of exposure to young interns
untrained to handle such losses.

Others, too, are wrapped up in this disease:
a friend, an aunt, or a mother.
They are using their bodies today
racing to the rise in the park toward
a view of Manhattan in a still blue sky,
the finish line nowhere in sight.

Harriet Susskind is a native New Yorker. She was educated at Hunter College, Ohio State University, and Syracuse University. Her poems have appeared in numerous journals and anthologies. Her book To See the Speech of Trees *was published in 1995. After a long academic career (and a longer running one), she still runs and writes.*

Claudia Sternbach

If I Were in Her Shoes

I see her as I drive through the village. She runs along the bike lane, her thick braid slapping her back, matching the rhythm of her stride. She lives in our neighborhood. I know she has at least one child. It doesn't seem that long ago that she was pregnant. But as I pass her on my way to return a video, or pick up a loaf of bread, I notice how strong her legs are. I envy what great shape she is in. And once more I promise myself that I will search through my closet for my old running shoes and hit the pavement.

I never was much of an athlete. I took up tennis in my early twenties, but loved hitting solid ground strokes more than actually competing. When facing an opponent across the net, my first instinct was to hit the ball right back to them. I enjoyed seeing how long we could keep up a rally; putting the ball away didn't often occur to me.

In softball, standing at the plate holding the bat over my shoulder, my palms would sweat, my heart pound. I would try to watch the ball as it approached and on those lucky times when I would hear the sweet sound of leather meeting wood, I was too surprised to sprint down the line. Needless to say I was never picked first to play.

But I always loved to run. It was such a pure and simple way to stay fit. And for the most part I only had to compete against myself. From my midtwenties until my early thirties I ran an average of fifty miles a week. I ran city blocks and country lanes. I looped around reservoirs and along freeways on narrow frontage roads. Every day I had to push myself out the door. The first couple of miles were the hardest. But then my legs would click into automatic, my breathing would become regular, and my mind would be free to wander.

For most of those years I lived in and around Berkeley. I would run up behind the Claremont Hotel, or through the Cal campus past the fraternity and sorority houses. Sometimes I'd run up to the football stadium and then on to the track where I could catch a glimpse of the bay.

Once in a while I would run with a friend. Mostly I ran alone, enjoying the solitude, the poetry of my surroundings.

Traveling didn't alter my schedule. My friend Cathie and I were in New York one year for the U.S. Open. She was playing. While staying with friends in Manhattan we would get up early enough to run through the city, ending up on the paths in Central Park. Hopping a fence, we once sat ourselves at a lovely table on the patio of Tavern on the Green, had an extravagant brunch.

Over the years I have racked up miles on the Yucatán Peninsula, in the Arizona desert, on the strip in Las Vegas. I've dealt with the altitude in Colorado and the humidity of New Jersey in the summer.

Then I got lazy and quit. I had wonderful excuses. My knees

started to bother me. I had a new baby. The hill by my house is so steep. But really, I was simply turning into a sludge.

My new baby is almost thirteen. Every once in a while I have made myself a promise to begin running again. I have driven down to the woods or to the beach and parked my car. I've stretched my calves while watching cyclists and runners pass by. And I have actually run a mile or two. And felt great. But within a few weeks my running shoes once more made their way to the back of the closet.

Yesterday morning I tried to attack the pavement with enthusiasm. A slight drizzle began, my knees began to grind, and fifteen minutes later I was nursing a latté while trying to convince myself that running was a part of my past for good. Who could be expected to hurdle these obstacles?

In the evening I drove over to my friend Amber's house to pick her up for a party we were going to. She climbed in my old Trooper and gave me a hug. Her big, curly hair framed her smiling face beautifully.

"Guess what happened to me at Costco this week?" she asked.

I shrugged.

"My foot broke," she said, but began to laugh.

At first I though she meant the foot she had been born with, her "real foot." But no, it was her "plastic foot," the one she has relied on for years since the car accident.

"I went to my doctor," she continued. "He told me it would be weeks before I could get a replacement. Weeks. I didn't know what I would do. But then he looked in his closet. There was a foot. A spare. And it fit my shoe. Worked perfectly. Can you believe how lucky I am. Can you believe it?"

I adore perspective.

I got up and ran this morning. My knees were creaking. My skin jiggling. My lungs straining. One hip felt slightly askew.

It wasn't easy.

But who ever said life was a walk in the park?

Claudia Sternbach is a newspaper columnist and freelance writer living in northern California. She has been published in the anthologies, Storming Heaven's Gate *and* In Celebration of the Muse, *and the journal* Quarry West. *Her book* Now Breathe *(Whitaker Press) was published in 1999.*

C. J. Lockman Hall

Running in the New Year

This race was a milestone. I had not been able to participate in any sweat-breaking activity since two disks in my upper back had become agitated eight months earlier. Now I was psyched to run in the New Year's Eve 5K in Nags Head, North Carolina.

"Rest," the physical therapist had said. "It will take time to heal and you can't hurry the process." Thank goodness I had an excuse for shirking leaf-raking responsibilities, but all other activities I yearned for.

Swimming, my main form of exercise, was too painful unless I could finish an hour-and-a-half practice without turning my head to breathe. Cycling? I was instructed to keep my head over my shoulders to improve posture and keep my weight evenly distributed—not exactly an aerodynamic position. Weight lifting? Some of the muscles affected by the disks were being strengthened by tossing around two-pound dumbbells that felt *really* heavy. Even running produced too much jarring for comfort. Okay, dancing lessons could continue. However, after a whirlwind evening of hustle, tango, and cha-cha practice, I could barely lift my arm to drive home.

With my willing mind frustrated by an ailing body, athletics lost their charm and allure. Wow, the professional performance motivator and positive thinking advocate not interested in exercising? This wasn't an ideal situation.

My husband saved my sanity (and his) by walking with me. We faithfully strolled the neighborhood streets every night, even when he arrived home from sports practice at 10:30 P.M., with dinner yet to be eaten (bless his heart). Can't complain, I thought, at least I can do something; my parents walk two miles every day, and they are quite fit. We began to enjoy and depend on those walks, sleeping restlessly on the rare evening we missed. How it did not rain at night for six months straight, I'll never know, but we were blessed.

We continued our walks during a relaxing week at the Nags Head beach house on the heels of a hectic holiday season. After a few dreams about pain-free exercising, I realized my body was ready to handle more. Since I was still incapable of swimming, I decided to jog.

Maybe it was the sixty-five-degree air, the ocean breeze, the wide, flat open roads; maybe it was that my sweat was like priceless perfume, but it was great! I could jog! Jogging slowly the next few nights, my body reminded me that it was definitely in charge of pace and distance, and I respectfully listened.

The New Year's Eve 5K race, an annual event for us, was rapidly approaching. Sensing that my competitive juices were beginning to flow, my husband reminded me that if I insisted on running in the race, I was to take it easy. Giddy at the prospect of my athletic rebirth, I instantly agreed.

We arrived at the restaurant hosting the race and greeted the owner, who was joining his wife in her first-ever race. Other entrants in this unique road race ranged from a trio pushing a baby carriage with a nice-sounding stereo system, to a champion runner, to a woman with her thirty-five-mile-per-hour greyhound hoping for a best time (for the woman, not the dog), to walkers out for exercise.

As we lined up at the start, I realized that the temperature had plummeted twenty degrees and the ocean breeze was whipping up, its dampness and strength able to penetrate a coat of steel (not to mention my coat of fleece). As the race started with a "Ready? Go!", the wind was at my back, lulling me into a false sense of "Hey, this isn't so bad!" Then I turned the corner into the headwind but barely noticed because I was so glad to be running. As the racecourse snaked by our beach house, I shed my now-too-warm coat in our driveway, drawing perplexed giggles from the crowd.

Rounding the final turn, asthma and tightness reared their ugly heads. I had not experienced these physiological "treats" for so long that I (almost) welcomed them. Chanting in time with my paces, I repeated, "You are tough and are almost there!" With the finish times called out by moonlight, my husband informed me that I had bested my PR—set on a warm, windless summer day—by a minute and a half!

While I changed my clothes in the restaurant parking lot in the middle of a cold and windy night, I felt like I was in paradise. I felt like I had won an Olympic gold medal.

I have learned not to despair. I know better days are coming. I try to keep moving forward in one way or another. I believe even my light walking kept my body used to daily physical activity, smoothing the way for my delightful reentry into the competitive athletic world.

I don't take my workouts for granted anymore. I am grateful for even my "worst" workouts, because I know someone, somewhere, is yearning for those athletic feelings.

Wave to me on the trails, or on the roads. I'll be the one stretching . . . and smiling.

C.J. Lockman Hall is a devoted amateur athlete, freelance writer, and motivational speaker. Her articles on sports performance and the joy of sport have appeared in a variety of magazines. She received her undergraduate degree from Princeton University and her masters in sport psychology from University of Maryland–College Park.

Jan Priddy

Runner's High

When I was forty-one I began running—not a slow comfortable jog, but serious running, training. My mother often says wryly that when the urge to exercise comes over her she sits down until it goes away. For most of my life I followed her lead. I walked miles in college only because I had to. I did not seek out opportunities to sweat. Four years ago this changed.

My older son and two of his friends had been running with the high school cross country team since they were in seventh grade. Alan was not the one the coaches were after. They had their eyes on Jasper and Bowen who were built lean and leggy like runners. Alan was simply determined and he liked running. Alan and the other two boys took the bus from middle school to the high school (where I teach) and I hung around after my classes during the cross-country season. For two seasons I'd walk out and watch practice, my son with the older kids and his faster buddies. I watched Alan put in strong, though rarely competitive, runs. One coach told me his determination was going to serve him well in life and I thought, yes it will.

So the spring before my son entered high school I decided to start running myself. I began on April Fool's Day, a sort of joke on myself. I expected my knees to give out, my joints to insist I stop this foolishness. Except for my horsy period in preadolescence, I have never been remotely athletic. I ran the mile once in high school because I was required to, three minutes behind the girl in front of me.

So there I was at forty-one unable to manage a quarter mile. My son was playing coach that first day, giving me tips about form and unable to grasp just how dreadfully out of shape I was.

"You're kidding," he said as I slowed to a walk after a couple of blocks.

"I am an old woman and out of shape. Leave me alone!" I retorted. Our house fronts the ocean, a beautiful place to run. He ran on the beach south to the creek and back, a total distance of about a half mile. I couldn't manage it.

It took until May to hit a mile, nearly eight weeks. By then my body seemed to figure out what I was asking for. I trained on wet sand during low tide, and by July I could make it to the town north of us. Six miles every other day in about an hour. I'm hooked.

There was no girls' cross-country team when I was in high school. Even if I'd been interested there wasn't a coach in my high school who would have taken the time to talk to me. I waited twenty years for a reason to get me running. What got me going was watching my son keep at it despite the fact that he wasn't going to win. I admire that kind of grit. Sometimes, in the winter off-season, Alan and I run together. He runs four miles for my three, and sometimes I run hills on the highway while he runs the beach, but

I still feel we're in it together. In the summer, when I'm not in class, while my son is counseling at camp, and before I begin my day of classes and errands, I run.

I start the cross-country season in better shape than most of the students, and though by season's end in November I am slower than some, I can keep going longer than all but a few. I can go the distance. In August 1996 I first ran in the Hood to Coast Relay from Mount Hood to Seaside, Oregon. Twelve thousand runners in teams of twelve cover 195 miles. It is the largest relay in the States. Our team is not competitive; the members include local men and women from their teens to their late fifties whose goals are similar to mine. We want to have done it. My three legs totaled 16.2 miles, and I ran in ninety-six-degree heat and in the dark that first year. I came away with four days of sore muscles and a huge sense of accomplishment. I find I am physically tougher than I knew.

In the past four years I have run nearly every week, three to five times, a total distance of fifteen to thirty miles. I have endured shin splints, a bruised heel, and occasional soreness. Two falls ago my younger son entered high school and joined the cross-country team. All three of us! Except Ian is fast, much faster than either Alan or I. And he doesn't care that much for running; it's just something he's good at. Unlike Alan and I who must train most of the year to stay strong, Ian seems to have been born that way.

This summer after his graduation, Alan and I train together for the Hood to Coast Relay, my third outing and his first. Next fall my younger son, built lean and strong like a runner, will probably be the fastest runner on the boys' cross-country team, Alan will be away at college, and I will be coaching the girls' cross-country team.

All of these are outward goals, but that they happen at all has less to do with yearly competition than daily need. I run for the high, the accomplishment, and somewhere at the base of it, because I am too impatient to walk. I want speed, but more important than that, I want the routine run, the routine that includes forcing myself to do something I still cannot quite believe I do, to push myself someplace slightly beyond where I think I want to go, and to come back feeling glorious and glowing because it's done.

I'm up at six and running on the beach and the fog is just holding offshore, the sun announcing its intentions on the other side of the Coast Range, and I am running hard, my T-shirt tucked into my bra, sweat running into my ears, and I see two crows and a raven picking a seagull carcass on the tide line. My watch tells me the first mile is too slow, and I pay attention. The first mile is my hardest and my left shin has a tiny flash of pain. Not shin splints, I decide. I check my watch at one and a half miles and it looks good. I push out with each stride, relax my hands, breathe steadily. The second mile is faster, enough faster to make me wonder again if my one-mile marker is really at the red beach stairs or three houses back at the A-frame house so that I'm timing it too long. I turn at Hug Point, my two-mile marker, and head home. The thick sea air drags in my throat and I think about the high school cross-country coach warning about "sucking air." That's what it feels like I'm doing, sucking in that wet breath.

I'm on my last mile and my watch tells me I need to hustle to make my time so I kick it in, just enough to maintain my pace. It always takes more effort on the way home to hold steady, but I'm grinning—runner's high, which for me happens after three full miles. A bubble of joy ripples up from my gut. Whatever hurts, I don't mind.

The raven is gone, but the crows are still pecking away. I pound straight through the creeks, no fancy prance over deep spots, but straight through. My shoes are heavy now with water and I'm feeling strong. I look ahead, trying to gauge where on the beach my run ends, at the second bend of wet sand or the third. There will be another bend I can't see until I get closer, but I check my watch and begin my final sprint anyway. I want to be done, but I try not to think ahead of where I am and what I need to do now. I don't fuss about whether I can kick in this early and not collapse. I tell myself the finish is the nearest dark loop of tide-washed sand and I know I am lying but I'm running too hard to pay attention to what I'm thinking. I look up the beach to count houses, a hundred meters, fifty, forty, no, forty more. I swing my arms high forward on each stride, sprinting. And then I'm done, past the imaginary mark on the sand in front of my house where I'm allowed to stop. I stop.

I turn away from my course toward the sea, gasp, and bend over for a three count. Sea air fills my mouth, head, throat, perhaps down to my knees. I walk south again past my house, straightening my body and breathing deeply, raw air deep into my chest. It does get better than this.

In the house, I take two aspirins, two glasses of water, a hot shower with a citrus soap and shampoo, pad barefoot to the bedroom, put on a favorite blue cotton turtleneck and my old jeans. They are loose over my hips and I go back downstairs to pour myself a cup of coffee, opaque in my glass mug, and walk back outside to the deck where I sit on top of the picnic table and look at the surf. Think about the run, the distance, the time, my goals for the week. This is easy, routine. My breathing stills. This is when all is right with the world. Hot coffee cradled in my palms and the beautiful view. Heat pours off my skin from my run, creating an envelope of comfort within the dawn chill. The weathered table is hard beneath me and I place my shoes side by side on the bench, squeeze my knees together, and look west beyond the narrow yard. My elbows rest on my knees and I take a cautious sip of coffee because it is too hot to drink, but cooling in the air. My body still feels the sting of exercise and that afterglow from exertion beyond comfort, from pushing myself to beat my own time. This feeling will last most of the day.

The day is perfect, the routine feeds me. I have time to slow down after all that hurry, a little drunk from exertion. Notice, I remind myself gently. If I forget, I might never run so hard, might never pause to watch the same sea I admire daily, and I might not notice the good life while it's happening. Like right now.

I have run at dawn and in the dark, over gravel, sand, and concrete, through gale-force winds, heat at noon, and driving hail. I don't necessarily recommend all these experiences, but I am grateful to have had every one.

When I get the urge to exercise these days, I sit down afterward. First I go out for a run.

Jan Priddy teaches English and coaches cross country on the northern Oregon coast where she lives in her great-grandaunt's house. She is a licensed field trial judge for sighthounds and has written for Sighthound Review, Afghan Hound Quarterly, *and the* Gazehound. *She also reads and writes herself breathless.*

Nancy LaMar Rodgers

On the Soles of Angels

The old man asked me what I was running from. I was in full stride so I couldn't slow down to answer him. I could only hope that the wind carried my correction of "running toward" to his ears.

It had been two years since I lost my sister to breast cancer. Her death had followed that of my best friend, whose death had followed that of my mother. Their unfathomable exits from my life left me anesthetized. I became barren and unoccupied, a remnant. Exercise, like so many of the other joys in my life, fell away. Food became a savior, a friend, a comfort. I crammed whatever I could down into that canyon of dull aching.

My daughter was four months old when I realized I could no longer blame the extra thirty pounds that sat around my midsection on the trials of being a new mom. More than just feeling the physical restrictions that were now placed on my body, I was ashamed of my stagnation. I had become sluggish, inept. The pounds crept on like mire, pulling me under slowly. I didn't care that my clothes didn't fit. I didn't care about anything. I had become an engorged shadow of my former self.

"Maybe you should go for a walk," my brother suggested, while I sobbed to him over the phone. It would have been my sister's forty-fourth birthday. "It's beautiful out tonight. Go. It will make you feel better," he said.

I hung up the phone and told myself he was insane if he thought a stroll around the block would alleviate my pain. I would placate him and go for a walk, and I would tell him how wrong he had been.

The October air was animated. The trees swayed with colored ornaments that whispered and crackled. The sun was at that perfect spot in the sky where it created a kaleidoscope. I headed down toward the water. I would watch the sun begin its slumber over the Long Island Sound. I walked about half a mile when I began to feel winded. I knew going back was uphill, and how would I make it?

Half a mile, I thought, how insulting. I had always been athletic. I walked a little longer. The path along the water was a mile long. It would be getting dark. I should head back. I would start out earlier tomorrow.

With that one confirmation stuck in my head, I did head out earlier the next morning. I walked the entire length. For two weeks I walked that path, every day. It was the first time that my reminiscences were not interrupted by the daily routine of work and family. The evenings started turning colder. It would be November soon, and the holidays would be upon us. I no longer looked forward to them. They were just reminders. There would always be empty chairs at the Thanksgiving table, and Christmas would blister my heart with its rejoicing.

As I headed out I knew I had underdressed for my walk. I was cold. Perhaps I should just go back; curl up with a blanket, a box of chocolate, and a good book. I turned around and the wind smacked me in the face. Like a chastised child I felt a sudden welling of indignation. It was a brief moment on that frosty autumn evening that altered me, a perfect instant as crystal as the night air. I would not go home. I would not go gentle. I would not go soft. I picked up my pace instead. I swung my arms. My legs were now jogging. I warmed up in minutes. In less than half a mile, I removed my outer sweatshirt. The heated icy sting on my face was the reminder that I had won that night's battle.

In the next two months I would become obsessed, a soldier. I was up to two miles of jogging and power walking. The clothes were getting looser as the nights were getting longer. I ran a full four miles after three months; it was my thirty-fourth birthday. I felt the high. I remember my legs gliding, liberated. They carried my body through slush and they laughed at the wind when I turned the corner into its gale force.

The pounds came off quickly. I was shedding. It took about six months to melt away years of rage and anguish. There are still days when the sadness and emptiness bear down mercilessly; days that force me to climb. I run often. I take a different path whenever possible. I inhale my surroundings and exhale whatever ails me. The air on my face and the grass, cement, or sand beneath my feet, propel me forward.

I always run alone. I need nothing more than my thoughts and memories. I no longer wallow in the moroseness that once consumed my life, but rather am grateful for the healthy legs and heart that pound steadily. As I run toward the water, the next hill, or the sunset, I see the women who have passed before me, as guides and guardians, angels that have strapped a pair of wings to my ankles and sent me out to fly.

Nancy LaMar Rodgers is a thirty-five-year-old mother of one, who runs and writes in southern Connecticut. She is also a freelance make-up and wardrobe stylist for film and television who is currently working on her first full-length screenplay.

Kris Whorton

On Running a Hundred Miles in Virginia

For some time now, three years maybe, the idea of running a hundred-mile race has hidden in the curls of my brain. It was my father-in-law and the other participants of the Leadville 100 who put it there. Surprisingly, the "idea" of running a hundred miles didn't frighten me. Instead, it awakened in me a curiosity, a wonder in myself, my ability, my strength, both physical and mental, and a quiet want. As with the idea of running a marathon six years earlier, I felt no panic, no immediate need to set a date or start training toward the "goal." I simply let it live inside me for a while, months, a year, two years, until I felt it coming out as stronger than just a murmur.

My husband and I said we would do it together. Once the wonder and want became a voice, after a year of serious training behind me and enough runs over fifty miles, I let it speak. I had learned something with each run: my weaknesses and the ways I tried to make the hours pass more quickly by planning what I would do when I finished or the way I felt impatient to be done, angry and cranky and sick of myself. There were also the quiet ways I settled into myself, where I learned my strengths and the rhythm of my tired muscles, the sleeplessness of my bones, the many shades of a blue sky, the quiet life of alpine forget-me-not and the smell of sun-warmed pine. I learned my husband's strengths and weaknesses too and saw deeper into the pools of his calm and kindness.

We chose our race, we prepared for it, and when the day came, we stood quiet in our hearts with our hands clasped as the race director blessed us. We set out in the dark with a hundred or so other seekers. In that dark Virginia morning, a quiet hum started inside my heart and carried me as we ran on road for a few miles, flashlights bobbing, the air fresh and damp. We left the road for the first of many trails, across rocks and tree roots, higher and higher toward a sky that slowly lightened but never turned blue. The day passed in a cloak of dove gray, no sun, no rain, just rare glimpses from the top of Massanutten Mountain to the brown Shenandoah winding below through fields so green they seemed almost a dream.

My muscles tightened and relaxed and sweat covered me until the mosquitoes left me alone and the flies came, perhaps thinking I was something that had died. Blisters formed between and under my toes, at the edge of my heels, along the balls of my feet, each one seeming to find sharp rocks until the force of my weight and the pressure of being pinched made them pop. With that, my day seemed much brighter.

My husband paced the first half, leading steadily through the aid stations where we picked up water and our powdered food, through mile after mile. I followed patiently, my brain quiet. I knew that later, when his energy stores ran out and his body moved beyond fatigue, my brain would have to be clear so I could lead us. It would be dark then and we would have at least sixty miles behind us. We might be tired of running, tired of the trails, tired of our food and our shoes and our stink but still there would be too many miles and a whole dark night ahead of us. There would also be mountain laurel and wild azalea lining the trail, making clouds of sweet escape and cool streams to cross, to dip our bandannas in and be refreshed. There would be dirt roads for easy running and a break from hills and rocks.

Night came as we walked hand in hand on a quiet dirt road along a creek. I felt calm and happy, no hurry to be anywhere else, no worries about finishing. "We can do this," I said to myself and I realized I had never doubted it. We kept on, one foot in front of the other, back on the trails, darkness with the tiny beam of the flashlight and mostly silence. My eyes grew tired of trying to focus. My husband was quiet. Tired. There was nothing I could say. I wanted to sit or lie down in the cool wildflowers and sleep, if only for an hour. "You could set your alarm," my brain said. "You could sleep." But I saw us, come morning, curled up in the grass as runners passed us and somehow we would wake up and still have to finish.

So I kept quiet and we kept on, one foot in front of the other, running when we could, walking, moving forward, on and on and slowly the sky became dove gray again. We had a new day and we were closer to the end. We ran, we hiked, and tried to smile. We kept on with miles and minutes passing as the sun rose somewhere above us. Then we climbed our last hill, ancient and green, and saw the finish below, maybe three miles away, spreading as fresh as hope. My husband led, hungry to be done, to rest. My heart felt so full of miles, of night, and green, happiness and relief and success. I thought, "How blessed I am to breathe and run and live with all of my strength of body and soul and mind and to trust in myself that I am able. How lucky I am to have a love who is with me every mile, suffering and smiling, craving beer and a hamburger, a nap, a shower, sleep and peace, and clean clothes."

We ran up the pasture to the finish line, hand in hand. "I am so proud of you," my husband said. He squeezed my hand and smiled and the joy and sorrow I saw in his eyes matched how I felt about finishing my first hundred miles.

Kristine Whorton recently moved from Colorado to Huntsville, Alabama, where she is pursuing a master's degree in literature at the University of Alabama. She is working on her second novel and a collection of poetry. Ms. Whorton is an avid runner, rock climber, gardener, and all-around outdoor enthusiast.

Char Simons

Hot, Cross Buns

Buck naked. Two hundred bobbing butts jiggle as the starting gun goes off. Following a gravel road, we head out of the campground then turn east on a U.S. Forest Service trail. Up, up, up, the butts bob two and a half kilometers up Tiger Mountain, then down, down, down, appendages jiggle for another 2.5 kilometers to the finish line.

Six years—that's how long it has taken me to get the courage to join the bobbing butts at the annual Bare Buns Run. The race, staged at Fraternite Snoqualmie Nudist Park in the Cascade foothills outside Issaquah, Washington, is a chance for skin—and lots of it—to be sweetly kissed by the mild, midsummer sun and breezes of the Pacific Northwest.

Every January as I map out races to tackle for the coming year, I pencil in the Bare Buns Run. Every year, my friend Melody swears she will do it with me. "This will be our year," we pledge. Nights leading up to the race are filled with dreams of angst—of being the only one at the race with clothes, or the only one without clothes, or the only one shedding clothes partway through the competition. And every year, Melody backs out to go on an even wilder adventure, like running up Machu Picchu—but with her clothes on. So every year, I chicken out at the thought of doing the race among strangers.

So what is the big deal about running buck naked with a couple hundred other people? There may be some deep, hidden feminist significance to the dilemma. Perhaps the Madison Avenue/Hollywood conditioning of not being satisfied with fleshy bodies. Or the virgin/whore syndrome. Or Eve, the temptress, in the Garden of Eden. Whatever.

As a newspaper reporter, I once interviewed a nudist for a feature story. Jake arrived at Dancing Goats Espresso wearing clothes —and way too much cologne. A trainer at the local YMCA, Jake claimed he liked baring all just for the freedom and comfort of it. A few months later, he started doing naked Bible readings at midnight on the local public access channel. Too weird. Would Fraternite Snoqualmie be a park full of Jakes?

The atmosphere during the twenty-minute trip in the camp shuttle bus from the Issaquah park-n-ride off Interstate 90 is tense. We are all still dressed, as is Sam, our dark-haired, muscular guide, sitting up front with a microphone.

"Welcome to the sixth annual Bare Buns Run. How many of you are here for the first time?" he addresses the busload of runners.

Maybe a third of us admit to being rookies and meekly raise our hands.

"I'd like to go over some of the park rules," Sam continues.

No ogling, no unwanted touching. Carry a towel to sit on. The same conventions and manners that apply at other social gatherings, whether cocktail parties or employee picnics, apply here. Except that we will be naked. Buck naked.

We can keep our clothes on, Sam says reassuringly, but we will probably feel more comfortable "dressed" like everybody else. Margaret and I smile at each other nervously. A backup to Melody, who was off doing a 100K footrace on Mount Rainier, my colleague Margaret comes off as reserved and quiet. She has, however, an unfettered wild streak, which led her to sign up for the race without hesitation.

The men in the seats surrounding us look grim and silent, no more at ease than Margaret and I are. A few joke nervously. At the back of the shuttle bus are the veterans—a mom and her two elementary-school-aged children. Besides running gear, their swimsuits, towels, and inner tube suggest they know a secret about nudism that the rest of us have yet to discover.

Doing a bare buns run is a telling test of trust and friendship — and not just of your fellow racers. Who, among family, friends, acquaintances, and coworkers, is it safe to tell you've run in the buff? Like a lesbian who has yet to come out, bare buns runners are cautious about whom they share the experience with. You don't go blabbing about it to just anyone.

There is something to be said, however, for knowing whom you'll be bumping up against in competition. Nonchalantly, I queried members of the master's track team I work out with to find out if anyone was doing the race. An innocuous question from the local newspaper's weekly running/triathlon columnist. Could be a great story. Didn't fool anyone.

"Yeah, Turk's doing it. So are Cheryl and Steve. Why, are you?"

Descending from the shuttle in front of the Fraternite Sno-qualmie clubhouse, I try not to look around. I don't want to see Turk, Steve, or Cheryl. The white, one-story clapboard clubhouse is like the pearly gates of heaven, with the scene on the other side just as unknown. Entering, you're dressed. Emerging, you're naked.

Eyes averted, I stride purposefully onto the grassy hillside near the start/finish line. I don't know what the swarm of people around me look like, but the grass is in good shape. Soft, smooth, green. Near the lawn bowling area is Margaret. Good thing she is sitting on the ground, a white towel beneath her, or I would have missed her. Like a handful of other women, Margaret—who is not much more endowed than I am—has kept her jogbra on.

As more of a distance runner, I need to warm up, so to speak, before the start of the 5K race. Trotting down the campground road wearing only socks, Asics, and a smile, my inhibitions melt under the noonday sun. Breezes and sunshine wrap around my body, including places that have never experienced the elements before. The rush of wind upon takeoff bathes my skin in a soft sheet of air, while the sun gently toasts me. A faint aura of sweat begins to form gently and uniformly on my skin—no soggy T-shirt on this run. All of a sudden, I can look people in the eye.

Close to race time, Margaret and I head back to camp and the starting line. Next challenge: to pack ourselves in among a couple hundred other naked runners. It's one thing ambling along alone or in pairs, like gazelles in the forest, supportive but without need or fear of touch. It's another to be wedged into a pack of boisterous, scrappy dudes and dudettes.

While almost everyone is naked, a few have donned even more creative race attire, like the two big, beefy guys wearing shorts with two cheeks cut out of the butt. Or the beefcake centerspread with a tiny tuxedo wrapped around his penis.

Bang! The starter's gun fires, and we are off. Or, rather, we are up. And down. Up and down, up and down. Those of us near the back of the pack jog in place, appendages bobbing, for a few seconds until the crowd spreads out. As the stream of runners turns onto the forest service trail and the two-plus kilometers of uphill, the raw spirit of competition spurs me to start acting like an athlete instead of someone caught with her pants down.

Twenty years of hill training, which sounds ominous and painful but really isn't, is paying off. At home in Olympia, the state capital, I seek out hills and trails. My worst training runs and races are on flat roads where the sense that I should be going faster than I am sets in. Hills and trails are more forgiving. Or rather, I am more forgiving of my modest running talents on more challenging terrain. The result of all that hill training is being able to charge up Tiger Mountain, leaving much of the pack "behind."

"Way to go, Char!"

Over my shoulder, I catch a glimpse of my track buddy Steve, urging me on. He, his wife Cheryl, and I bring up the rear at those Tuesday-night lung-busting interval sessions dominated by four-, five-, and six-minute milers. Steve usually saves his best for last, typically zooming past me on the last lap of the workout. As I continue chipping away at Tiger Mountain, I fully expect to see Steve again—this time from behind—dashing past me right before the finish line.

Up the dusty trail I continue picking off runners. Before long, only two women remain ahead of me. Damn! I'd never considered the possibility of actually placing in this race. Feeling good, I finally succumb to curiosity and look at my watch. I used to be a real chronometer junkie, checking every mile split. As age and parenthood began slowing me down, I let go of the pressure of knocking milliseconds off and now only look at my watch for overall time.

Eighteen minutes, my purple Timex Indiglo registers. Eighteen minutes? We should have come to the turnaround point by now. Either that or I've really slowed down with old age.

"The turnaround's just ahead!" shouts a runner heading back down the mountain to the finish.

Being a good middle-of-the-packer, I faithfully follow the runners in front of me and turn around when they do. No cone or sign marks the spot, only a slight dip in the trail. Making the turn, I follow gravity's lead on the downhill and kick into high gear. Whizzing down the mountain, the small lead pack of bobbing buns I am following grows in number. As I turn off the trailhead and toward the finish chute, Steve guns past me. I expected that, but several women runners I'd passed on the way up Tiger Mountain, including Cheryl, are already milling around aid tables laden with postrace bottled water, bagels, and fruit. Hadn't I passed them? How did they finish before me?

"Bare Buns Run: 5K (or 6.14)" read the race results the following month in a regional running magazine. By accident or design, the turnaround marker had been knocked off the trail, leading the overzealous among us to overshoot.

Which makes a return appearance at next year's Bare Buns Run all the more likely. In the meantime, Margaret and I cast knowing glances at each other at the office whenever a topic even slightly related to nudity comes up. And Cheryl, Steve, Turk, and I have formed a small, close-knit circle among the track club. We are also busy recruiting trustworthy running buddies, who won't get us fired or arrested for our barable activity, to join us at next year's race.

Char Simons is a freelance journalist, communications consultant, and adjunct faculty member at the Evergreen State College, Olympia, Washington. She squeezes in running and triathlons between loving and laughing with her husband, Jeff Smith, and their two sons, Taylor and Mackey.

Jennifer Wheelock

Because They Can

The last mile of a ten-mile run can be trying. The knees get an arthritic ache. The hip joints hurt just enough that you imagine you actually feel the abrasive rubbing of the rotator cuffs. Your chiropractor warned you, and now your hips remind you that you ignored her admonitions to cut back. You picture the ball-and-socket joint, fear that this may be the moment it decides to lock up in protest. There's a bit of satisfaction too, of course, the runner's high that rewards those truly disciplined or truly obsessive enough to get through the first nine miles. But when you know ten is the end, you're just ready to get there. Every step resounds in your head like footsteps in a horror film, closer, closer, closer.

It was during such a mesmeric moment this morning that I met him. He was gorgeous, and as taken by my presence as I was by his. Few things stop me dead in my tracks during a run, but the sight of this ten-point buck did. Ten points, one for every mile this morning. Reward enough, I thought.

This was not the first buck I had seen hanging around the house. Since we moved to the farm several months ago, I've seen a few wild animals. A family of deer ran by our bedroom window one morning in April, graceful and gallant, like well-groomed parents with their children off to church on Easter Sunday. One morning at sunrise, as I ran down the dirt road that circles by our little farmhouse, a coyote bustled out of the scrub into the road ahead, on his way to the wood on the other side. Noticing one another, we both slowed our paces before quickening them and running in opposite directions. But for an instant, we stared straight one at the other. What did he see when it appeared he was looking into my eyes? How does a coyote perceive a person from ten feet away? Was my image as unclear to him as his way of life is to me? Why did I frighten him? Has he heard stories of my killer instinct, my penchant for hunting? I imagined he was late getting home from the nightly hunt, anxious to get cozy with his pups in a den deep in the pines, my way of giving purpose to his pace. For whatever reason, he ran away, and I ran on around the circular road.

Normally the canine types I encounter on my morning runs are dogs. Dogs are as common in rural north Florida as grit, many of them hunting dogs useful in designated seasons for tracking deer. Some of these are kept in pens, but most rarely see a fence or a runner, so when I run the roads that edge their property, I'm fair game. It's possible the only thing a dog likes to chase more than a car is a person running down the street. I should have some healthy fear of strange dogs, but I don't. When they romp toward me from their front porches, I talk to them, ask them their names, tell them how good they are to try to stave off a stranger such as I. Often when they hear my unintimidated tone, they stop, cock their heads, and prick their ears, as if they are wondering why they didn't recognize an old friend. Yesterday a rottweiler, some 150 pounds of black and tan muscle, ran at my heels for nearly half a mile. I urged him to keep up. "Just do it," I panted, but he gave out. Probably because he didn't have good running shoes. One time I did heed a prominent BEWARE OF DOG sign posted on a telephone pole at the edge of someone's property. It grabbed my attention because it was flanked by two other signs: NO TRESPASSING and BAD DOG—KEEP OUT. I heard a ferocious bark and so turned as I approached the edge of the driveway and ran back the other direction. As I did I looked over my shoulder with some perverse zoomaniacal desire to see the barking beast that had necessitated such warnings. There in the yard, barely discernible from my distance, was a miniature dachshund, probably a twelve-pounder, doing impressive fifty-yard dashes between two trees: back and forth, back and forth—his floppy ears seemingly doing as much to propel him as his stumpy legs. Each morning now, I run right on by that house. The dachshund and I both get a workout.

Perhaps what I love best about farm life is walking out my front door to a view of twenty cattle in the pasture across the dirt road from our front yard. The cows and bulls belong to Clyde, our landlord, and owner of the two hundred acres we inhabit and share with several dogs, four horses, five cats, a rooster, a rabbit, an unknown number of coyotes, deer, and armadillos, and these cattle. One of the dogs is our Labrador/Samoyed mix, Delta, a blond beauty with long hair and a curly tail. Until recently, Delta was a city dog, a suburbanite with a fence and a leash and a couch. More than any of our other dogs, though, Delta has taken to farm life.

When I let her loose in the mornings, she takes off like a horse out of the gate. She runs circles in the yard and around the house, chases Clyde on his tractor, or sprints to the pond a mile or so across the property. When she returns, prancing proudly back into the yard, she smells of stagnant pond water or rotting roadkill, but her upward chin and curled tail belie her dogness. She is a royal stallion, just run her course. One day while writing, I looked up from my computer and through the front window to see twenty heifers herding along the barbed-wire fence. Clyde does not herd his cattle and, having never before seen them move so methodically, I was puzzled by their strange behavior. Then I spotted Delta, dogtrotting along just outside the fence. When she reached the edge of the pasture on one side, she turned and ran the other way, pausing long enough to make certain the cows were coming too. All the while, she kept glancing toward the house, looking for me in the window, eager to show off her newly discovered, innate capacity for herding cattle, while twenty unamused cows worked off some hard-won pounds.

The most notable of Clyde's cattle is a two-thousand-pound (that's one ton, which means he could not safely cross some bridges) bull named Cowboy. Cowboy can't breed anymore, but Clyde keeps him around. He doesn't have the heart to have him slaughtered, and I am grateful for this fact. Whenever I need a miracle, a little proof that the impossible can happen, I watch Cowboy run. Really, it's more a gallumph than a run, but it is an amazing thing, and when it happens I envision disaster. Will there be an earthquake? Will his bony legs break under the shifting force of two thousand pounds of flesh and bone? Will the ground give way beneath his hooves, leaving four thin, deep holes in the field and a bull up to his belly in mud and dung? So far, no tragedy has come of Cowboy's barreling, but I wonder why he runs at all. It looks like it hurts, all that bulk bouncing, like running with packs of sand thrown over your back and shoulders. But he lumbers away, and the wind meets his huge brown eyes as he goes with really no place to go at all except maybe the pond or a different bale of hay or some grass that hasn't been chewed to the nubs. Usually he just makes circles in the pasture, or schleps short distances to nowhere, as if he's celebrating the good fortune of having bred enough to be useful without becoming a hamburger, and of belonging to a softy like Clyde who'll keep him around until he kicks with a gut full of green grass. When he's tired, he crumples, looking sad and satisfied, as cattle often do, into a reddish brown mound.

However little or however much I have in common with other species, it seems I share with them at least the love of running. Though I started running years ago to get in shape, as I'm sure neither Cowboy nor the coyotes nor the deer nor my dogs did, I continue running for other reasons. Yes, it makes me feel better. Yes, it's an adrenaline rush, but that's nothing I couldn't get from a good shot of epinephrine. There's something else. Am I running for something? From something? Is it just that it feels good to meet the wind?

This morning as I ran one of my routes, I took turns trying to embody my vision of Cowboy, running against logic, defying gravity, the deer, bounding beautiful through the woods, my dog, muzzle in the air, smelling home. I tried to make myself a metaphor for their movement, thought this could be the implicit comparison that would lead me to a reason for running. I could feel myself getting closer, closer, closer. And I remembered:

At night, very late at night, when nothing but black is visible in the brush and fields outside our window, the coyotes run in packs of ten or fifteen. Instinctively, they run and they howl. Because they can.

Jennifer Wheelock teaches writing and literature at Kennesaw State University. Her poetry has been published in several journals. Her short short story "Staring into Spoons" appears in the anthology Freedom's Just Another Word. *She received honorable mention in* Negative Capability's *1996 Eve of Saint Agnes poetry competition and was a finalist in the 1997* Spoon River Review *poetry competition.*

Karen Hall

Marathon Training at Ten Thousand Leagues Under the Sea

After years of running by fits and starts and sticking to a running program for at most two months, I found a running partner who was only slightly faster than I was and together we managed to run through the heat of the summer and into the fall. We had set a goal to complete a 10K race before the snow fell, and in November, in wind and flurries, I completed a 10K, the longest distance I had ever run in my life. At some point on the course when I was confident that I would cross the finish line, I told my running partner, who happened to be an ex-lover who had done her darndest to get me to be a runner, that I planned to run the Mountain Goat in the spring.

From the name you can guess there are a few hills in the Goat. My friend, knowing the course, my habits, and the difficulties of training for a spring race in central New York, didn't tell me I couldn't complete this race, but her tone of voice and her posture revealed her skepticism. If she thought I couldn't do it, by god I was going to do it. That spring I pushed the longest distance I had ever run in my life to ten miles. I had earned my T-shirt, but my shallow base, inexperience racing down hills, and sloppy form resulted in hip and knee soreness that prompted me to take the next month off.

By May I was running again, this time training for the Albany Freihofer's Women's 5K. Along the way I hit an emotional nadir. I had lived with chronic depression for approximately two decades, but in May I felt worse than ever. The only thing that made me smile during my weekend in Albany was the bumper sticker on someone's car: SAVE THE PLANET, KILL YOURSELF. I finished an uninspiring race, ate my cookies, and drove home.

But I kept running. What I couldn't see yet was that each day my depression would lift for a few hours in the morning right after I ran. Gradually the window opened wider and my mood would be lighter for half a day. In mid-June on Gay Pride Day a woman I hardly knew walked up to me and said I seemed really happy. I was shocked to think my depression was visible enough that members of the community who weren't intimate with me would notice its presence or comment on its absence. But she was right.

The process had been so gradual that I only noticed it when others brought it to my attention. That my depression had lifted was empowering and frightening at the same time. I ran compulsively as if the depression was right behind me. But I still needed the pressure of a race and the incentive of a T-shirt to stick to a schedule, so now I planned to run a half marathon in August. I stayed with my scheduled long runs even when my neighbor laughed at how long it took me to get them in. I was running a twelve-minute mile then, so runs over ten miles were a big time commitment.

When August arrived, I didn't want to break the rhythm of my program. I was happily and compulsively following Jeff Galloway's marathon program. So I skipped the half marathon and I set my sights on Columbus, Ohio.

Four years earlier I had lived in Columbus while a graduate student at The Ohio State University. My depression and indecision had prompted me to quit my doctoral program, and I had never been able to accept this decision comfortably. Returning to Columbus to run the marathon would be a kind of triumph and proof that I could gut something out, even if it wasn't a doctorate in English.

So I kept running. I ran 5Ks and long runs and weekly short runs. I trained and I raced alone. Few runners want to train for a marathon, and even fewer who do train want to run a twelve-minute mile. In September I ran a 14K in 1:26:30. I was thrilled but as I drove home from Utica, I could feel my body telling me I'd come down the hill too fast. My knee swollen and sore, I ran only once the following week. My housemate was a physical therapist and supportive of my running. She showed me exercises and stretches for my IT band and commanded that I ice far more.

The following Sunday I cried through a good portion of my twenty-two-mile-long run, too stubborn to stop. I turned my watch off at the end; four hours and twenty-five minutes. My entire body slumped, convinced I had just completed my marathon. I went through the next week running without my watch so I wouldn't panic that I was going slower and slower. I iced, poked, and massaged my knee, always trying to convince myself that it wasn't swollen, it always looked like that, I just had pudgy knees.

I ran another uninspiring 5K and three days later my cat died. A week later I skipped my long run, in retrospect one of the smartest moves in that training season.

One week before the marathon, I ran a 5K PR, 27:33. I managed to keep pace with a much faster friend, controlling my breathing and doubts by repeating my new mantra, "Everything I need is in my legs and in my heart." After one more light week of training, I traveled with friends to Columbus. After five hours, ten minutes, and seven seconds during which I stopped at three Porta-Johns, hugged one Elvis impersonator, and ran the last two miles in some pretty fierce discomfort, I crossed the finish line and hugged the woman who put the finisher's medal over my head.

Who would predict that a chronically depressed, sedentary lesbian would summon her will to rise from the couch and within a little over one year complete a marathon? But when I try to describe the difference running has made in my life, the only analogy that seems to do justice to my experience is a description of living life under water. There were times when I lay on the couch and imagined I was sinking into a muddy river bottom.

I began my running career under water with the heaviness of an unbelieving martyr; I was convinced chronic depression was my cross to bear throughout my life, and I was equally convinced there would be no promised land on the other side of my earthly journey. I can paint this self-portrait with ironic gentleness, but there was a time when shame, anger, and embarrassment led me to paint it derisively.

My underwater days taught me compassion and confidence. On

some days I like to pretend that I didn't climb out of the river but like Hercules diverted its path. On other days I think of myself as Achilles; my mother, however, forgot to hold my ankle, and she dropped me into the River Styx, where with the flexibility of a child I grew gills and took up residence. Occasionally I let myself think that the running helped stimulate a chemical change in my body, but I don't think this for long, because it makes me anxious about changes beyond my control that may occur in the future.

No matter how I tell the story, the lesson I always choose to carry from it is about learning to have faith in my own strength and endurance. This faith has recently enabled me to return to my graduate work and to stop training for my second marathon. I announced to friends that I understood strength at this moment in my life meant taking care of myself so that I could concentrate on my academic work. And it's with the grace and faith running has brought me that I walk through each day, confident that all I need is in my legs and in my heart.

Karen J. Hall is currently running in the streets of Syracuse where she attends Syracuse University, writes for the Syracuse Peace Newsletter, *and lives a full life in the open air.*

Rebecca J-M Pierre

White Heat

In high school Rachel often ran and ran around the house. Ran and ran, like a dog circles its place before settling down to sleep. She ran for blessing, ran to ward against curse. She ran for safety (The streets weren't safe. It was nearing dark. You can't run alone in the dark, her mother said). She and her four brothers had contests. Who could run fastest. Who could run ten times around fast, who twenty. Finding shortcuts, cutting across the porch, leaping bushes, the garden, the hose. And her mother indoors, inside the circling bodies, the pounding feet. These circling vultures (her children) running around and around her as she stood inside at the kitchen window, preparing a meal. Rachel stopped. Picked up a jump rope. Jumped, ten, twenty, thirty times. Click, click, click, the slap of the rope against the driveway. She tried it inside the garage, but the rope slapped the ceiling, click, click, slap. Inside to dinner, to a glass of cold water. Your cheeks are so red, Rach! Glancing in the mirror, rubbing them.

In college Rachel does go out running at night, then comes home to lie in the grass. Her father has taken her brothers out to dinner at McDonald's, but she has evaded him by going on a run.

Mosquitoes hum and poke her skin under the stars, the Big Dipper. She stretches out in the grass. It tickles the backs of her legs and leaves dew marks. The Dipper scoops the twinkling stars. Oh Dipper, scoop these mosquitoes. Light from the porch falls in a rectangle near her body. Inside, the steady shuffling of cards. She closes her eyes to her grandmother's voice, can see her knotted hands, texture of aged tree trunk, holding the white and red cards. She wields the cards in her curled tree branch hands. Does she know how to love a tree? Do I? She knows what it feels like to hug a tree, scratchy bark, too wide for arms to go around. She know what it is to squeeze a giant redwood, to feel its clay red bark. She learned how to love another, smaller tree, easier to get her arms around.

Bats swoop from treetop to treetop, parallel to electric wires. Dark shapes dip, sprinkling of stars, hum of car, slap of tires. She opens and shuts the door smoothly, ducks into the living room, then crawls in between the piano and a plant. Voices, Where is she? We brought her a burger. Her dad lumbers into the bathroom. She holds her mouth to keep from laughing and clutches a piano leg. Where is she? Her grandma, knotted branch, wonders.

The car motor fades away. Thump thump thump. She take the stairs three at a time.

Where were you?

Running.

Where to, running? She tears down the graveled side of the highway, racing the cars, the very corn leaves. Knee high by Fourth of July. Not even July yet. She races the furrows cut by tractor's sharp blades, races the blue botflies.

Almost to the firehouse. It shimmers, a misplaced desert mirage in the distance. The road shimmers, heat waving off the surface.

There. Firemen's heads turn as she shoots by, a cannonball, a firework. Do they want to put her out? The dog at the end of the street awakens and barks, startling her. Feet don't fail me now; she picks up the pace. Feet pound; heart races. Heart pounds; feet race. Safety yards later. Sun cuts a mirage through her head, pushes her repeat button. Home home home. Steady bending of gravel will to her tread. Home.

Where to? Slowed to a walk, blood beats wildly in her, the wings of a blood bird trapped in her skin. Where to?

Not there yet, she knows, I'm not there yet.

That summer Rachel house-sits for her friend Mary, who lives in an affluent suburb where couples are out grilling and walking with their kids. Often she takes off into the woods and circles the dirt paths around the lake. There she doesn't run into many couples, but she often sees a white heron standing alone in the shallow part of the inlet. She runs fast, whirring downhill like a large dragonfly, uphill she runs furiously, intent on getting where she's going, feeling her muscles taut, her breath tight, then a swoosh down, past a family walking; they are a blur, indistinct. The hum of insects like a second skin surrounding her, the air vibrating with their noise and her harsh gasps of breath. She doesn't take her Walkman into the woods onto the secluded path. She wants to be able to hear anything approaching through the leaves, the gurgle of small streams swirling with bubbles.

She has emerged from the sunshine, running onto the path into the cool shade, when she sees a flash of white in the stream, like a lost handkerchief or a piece of torn, bleached underwear, the sort her mother uses for a rag. She slows to a stop still breathing hard, sweat trickling down her forehead, into the center of her sports bra. Her shoulders are bare and freckled from sun. She retraces her steps back to the flash of white, looks into the stream, nothing. Then she raises her eyes to the tree and draws in her breath. There is an albino squirrel clinging to the bark, spread out as if it would fly. She stands watching it, when there is another flash from the ground. Another white squirrel, stark against the dirt of the bank, the green weeds. She feels lucky, as if she has been shown these two for a reason, as if they are spirits, ghosts from another world, here to teach her a lesson.

Often, when she runs that path she sees the white squirrels; they stay in the same spot in the stream, clinging to the tree, rooting the bank for food. She wonders if they will survive the winter, whether they blend in with the snow.

Rebecca J-M Pierre has an M.F.A. in poetry and fiction from the University of Minnesota. Her writing has appeared most recently in Oxford Magazine *and* U.S. Catholic. *She recently ran her first 5K race in 24:12.*

Nelinia Cabiles

The Language of Feet and Hands

I ran in the dark, not quite trusting my feet. The unmarked trail to Hale Hina, the highest point on Lana'i, looked unfamiliar as I made my way past guava trees and noni, whose leaves my Apo Gina would grind into a poultice for deep wounds. Growing up, I recalled loving the smell of my Apo Gina's hands, stained indelibly from herbs and roots of plants.

I held my breath as I entered the forest. After eight years of being away from my childhood home, I was not surprised, though not completely prepared, for my disorientation.

The trail grew muddy and narrow and I almost lost faith that my memory would be complete enough to guide me in that uncertain light of dawn when shadows were blue and slippery and unreliable. But around the curve, I found the marker indicating I had two miles left to Hale Hina: a sodden tree stump, which looked like a child crouching in the dark, ready to spring in the air. I pushed through the overgrowth, my step suddenly light.

I had considered asking my sister Isabella to join me that morning, but decided she preferred sleep over an early-morning run, having arrived from Colorado the night before.

"Yes, let her sleep," my husband Billy had agreed. "It's a long flight from Denver, and Isabella mentioned last week that she'd been feeling tired lately. But she did say that during the last mile of our interval training, come to think of it, so maybe that was just an excuse. I *was* riding her pretty hard up the trail."

I watched my husband smile as he recalled the memory.

I walked to where he stood by the hotel room's large window and leaned against him.

"Billy," I said. I reached around him and tugged at the loops of his jeans, drawing him close to me. He stroked my shoulders, but his touch was absentminded, the tips of his fingers skimming my skin in broken figure-eights and loops.

I watched a wave surge past the fringe of black lava beds along the beach, then empty into dark pools. Wave after wave rose and retreated until the bay became a hollowed-out bowl, the water an indeterminate weight.

"That feels good, honey," I said, after a time. My voice broke our quiet into blank, windowless rooms. Billy's hands flew up like startled birds. "Billy?"

"Oh. Rennie. Sorry," he said. "Forgot where I was for a minute." I sensed his fingers floating above my shoulders, then felt him step away from me. "Well," he said. "Well. We should start thinking about dinner."

I felt my face grow hot, my hands damp and singed, as though I had stood too close to a burning lava field. I did not turn my head to follow him out of the room, but heard the solid click of the bathroom door as it closed.

I held my gaze out into the flat, indifferent sea, diminished in the late afternoon.

Billy had promised that he would make the run with me to Hale Hina that morning, but he had already left by the time I awoke, his running shoes gone. He had not left a note.

Hanae Abando, the front desk clerk and a former high school classmate, said she saw Billy in the lobby about an hour earlier, at 4:30 A.M. "Your husband? Tall guy, yeah? Dark wavy hair? Hmm." She appeared to give this some thought. "He didn't look like he was going running, Rennie, that's for sure," she said, twitching her lips and cocking her eyebrow in either sympathy or pity or malicious delight—I couldn't tell which.

"Okay," I said. "Thanks."

"Sure, sure," she said. "Glad I could help."

"I'd like to leave him a note, in case he gets back while I'm running."

"For sure," she said, handing me a pen and a notepad. "I'll keep my eye out for him. Here you go."

I cupped my hand over a corner of the pad and began writing.

"Long time no see, Rennie. Welcome home."

I looked up to see the corners of her mouth curl slightly, though her tone remained bright, helpful—the measured kindness of salesmen and real estate agents. Hanae and I had never been friends.

"Thanks. It's good to be back." I left her with a note for Billy to please remember we were meeting Isabella and King for breakfast at Apo Gina's.

Isabella and I ran Hale Hina's mountain trail more than a dozen times that year, the year my mother died of cancer. We left before dawn and made it home before our father could miss us or even know we were gone. Eight miles, round trip. I was nine, Isabella twelve. The distance between things never seems so remarkable when you're running away.

We would find our way to Hale Hina's pools below the falls, crawl up the ridge, clamber up the sprawling guava tree, and wait for the sun. We watched the sky open shyly, an arching flower, the valley below revealing itself to us in the growing light.

Isabella would perch on a branch near to mine, close enough so that she could scrawl letters on my back. It was a bedtime game we played until we fell asleep, afraid as we were of the approaching darkness. I would guess what words she was spelling as her fingers flew fast over my shoulder blades in her shorthand script:

B-U-T-Y-F-U-L, she spelled once, pointing to the sunrise.

Bella, I giggled, you're such a terrible speller.

I—pause—N-O, she answered, thumping the center of my back with the heel of her hand for comic effect.

The branches of the guava tree bent over with our laughter. I remember once, once, when we found ourselves at the Hale earlier than we expected to, and sat through the terrible quiet we would sometimes find there, Isabella spelled our mother's name in a flowing script from the top of my shoulder to the small of my back:

L-I-A-N-A, L-I-A-N-A.

Oh, Bella, I started to say, please, please don't, but she narrowed her eyes and put a finger to her lips.

M-O-M, she spelled. I-M-I-S-S-M-O-M.

M-E-2, I wrote back. S-O-M-U-C-H.

And we talked back and forth like that without stopping, finding all the words I did not know I had felt or understood, my sister patient and silent, her hands covering her face, transcribing under her breath, until my index finger began to cramp, until the sun burned through the fog, until I felt empty and wild all at once and didn't know whether I wanted to scream or let myself cry into the dark green cathedral of trees and flowers and leaves and so much earth. And before I could decide, Isabella flicked her wrist, tapping the face of her watch, a gesture that meant it was time for us to leave before we were late for school.

That morning was the closest I would ever feel to Isabella, suspended as we were above the ground, sharing a private language, joined by a nameless hurt, our words scored into our skin. Once I felt Isabella's hand touch my face, but the gesture happened so quickly, half of a breath it seemed, that I knew I could only have imagined it.

I thought of Isabella as I leaned into the steep rise, keeping my eyes focused three feet ahead of me. I counted my breaths to one hundred, each breath four strides, and knew that I had a mile of incline left. I thought of how she and Billy had become running partners over the past year. It was my idea, but I could not remember who set it in motion.

Isabella had said she could help Billy prepare for the Pike's Peak Marathon, having run it for the past three years. I pushed Billy to take her up on her offer. She can be a great coach, I told him. You'll be in top form in no time. Billy had been reluctant, but after a couple of weeks of training runs together, he agreed they had similar running styles.

You were right, he said, I feel like a different man. Isabella is amazing. She knows how hard to push and when to let up. She's got great timing.

Secretly, I had hoped that if she were Billy's coach, we would see each other regularly, making time for each other, the way sisters do. But it hadn't worked out that way. Isabella had always seemed too busy to get together.

Billy was ecstatic when he finished the marathon under four hours. We'll shoot for 3:30 next year, Isabella had told him. Or maybe even 3:15! Think of it, Billy.

As if the time itself, three hours and fifteen minutes, had a power in and of itself to transform them.

I would look forward to seeing Isabella every Saturday and Sunday after their long mountain trail runs in Boulder. Can you stay awhile, I'd always ask her.

I wish I could, Rennie, she would often say, but King's probably missing me already.

I've missed you, Bella, I wanted to say.

Once I asked if I could join them. "On long runs," I said,

"maybe once a month or two?"

"Billy and I run at a pretty fast clip," Isabella had said, "and we crank up hills."

"Oh, I can crank," I said.

"Really? Since when? What's your best time for a 10K? What did you run in the Bolder Boulder last year?"

"I'm not sure. I think forty-one something."

"Is that right?"

"Yes, I think so. But you know I don't keep track of those things. You know why I run. Because it's fun; because I need it. I sort things out in my head when I run."

"Rennie, Rennie," she said, snapping her fingers, impatient now. "I'm not trying to brush you off, but I take running very seriously. I always have. I'm hoping for a PR in this year's Garden of the Gods ten-miler. And besides, we just don't click when it comes to running. Remember high school cross-country?"

I remembered she had resented me for weeks for trying out for the team and making it. "As far as I'm concerned, Rennie, you're just another girl on the team. You're not my sister. You're not a friend," she said, counting off the reasons on her hand. "Don't expect me to be nice just because we're related."

"I know, Bella. Wasn't expecting anything."

"Don't you forget it," she said.

But when she was voted captain of the girls' team, she made it her goal to ignore or ridicule me. I tried not to let it get to me. I remembered our mornings at Hale Hina and knew that my sister loved me, in that grudging way of sisters.

"Move it, Rennie. Move your fat *okole!* I'm coming up from behind you!" she'd yell, as we began our ascent to Hale Hina, the switchback trail dusty until the last two miles when the path slipped into the rain forest. "Look up so you know what's ahead."

"I'd rather be surprised," I said, trying to keep up with Bella by controlling my ragged breath. "I don't want to know how much longer this hill is. I know I'd just give up. I know it. All I need to know is what's three feet in front of me. Much easier that way."

"Don't be stupid," she said, pushing the pace, sidestepping me as she took the inside path. Her elbow jostled my arm and we fell into an uneasy rhythm, her stride quickening, mine long and fluid. "Your body already knows, Rennie. Two miles, eight miles, uphill, downhill, *manini* easy, break-your-ass steep—if you've done it, your body never forgets. Look up. Trust me. I know these things."

Then, as if to prove her point, she raised her head even higher, kept her step light, and surged forward.

But I couldn't run that way, no matter how hard I tried. In all the island meets that year and the next three years, I'd run the hills by counting each yard with a measured breath, keeping my head down and bent to the wind, my hands loose, expecting nothing. If a hill took forty breaths to run, I knew I'd have to sprint down it in less than half the total count in order to make good time.

"Who taught you that? *That's* not a strategy," Isabella had sneered.

"Made it up. No one's technique but mine. It works for me. You know, just an instinct I have."

"Trust me, you won't win races that way. Your instinct stinks," she said, talking into the wind, away from me.

During high school, we grew far apart, traveling an unspooling line in my worst dreams, she and I on opposite ends, her face becoming as indistinct as my mother's until I could barely recall it.

I ran hard, feeling stronger with each step. By the time I made it to the top of Hale Hina, morning peeked over Maui. I looked west toward Kalani Bay. I thought of Billy and wondered if he had run there instead. I wondered whether he'd get my note. I wondered if he and Bella were running together that morning. I wondered, too, about the furtive silence that had crept between us over the past year. Ignored, it had become profound and intractable. It had been there the morning of our anniversary.

"Mmmm . . . waffles. With pecans and whipped cream, no less. If I didn't know you better, Billy, I'd say this was a kind of peace offering. Feeling guilty about something?"

"Guilty?" he said, scowling. "It's a little early in the morning to be so suspicious, don't you think? Did you forget it's our anniversary, Rennie?"

"No, I didn't," I said. "Hey, I'm sorry. You just took me by surprise. I didn't expect you home. You're usually running about this time. Damn. I'm sorry, Billy. This . . . this is nice. Thank you, and thank you for remembering."

He ran his fingers through his hair then crossed his arms over his chest.

"I'm sorry," I said again. "Happy anniversary."

I sensed something slide and shift in the room.

"What's going on," I finally asked. "Is something going on? It's not just this. I mean, I feel like you're so far away these days. Like we're running in the dark and I know you're out there because I have a sense of you, and I can almost hear you, but I keep missing you. We keep missing each other. Billy?"

He reached for his coffee mug.

"Don't you think we need to talk? This is the first time I've really seen you in a week. What is it, Billy? What?" I felt I might cry, so I squeezed my index finger and bit my lower lip.

His face softened. "I'm just feeling overworked, Rennie. I'll be fine once these conferences are over—you know the kind of preparation involved for these lectures. In two weeks, I'll be myself again. I promise. You won't know what to do with me I'll be around so much."

"I'll come with you," I blurted. "It'll be good for us to get away. And maybe we can squeeze a quick visit to Lana'i? It's only a half hour flight from O'ahu. I haven't been home to see my Apo Gina in ages."

"Are you serious? You said you were swamped at work with the new account," he said. "You said the client needed a lot of hand-holding."

"It'll be fine. The client will be fine. We hired a new AE and I've been handing off a small chunk of the project to her over the past month. Besides, the campaign doesn't kick off until October. That's two months away. Listen, I've accumulated three weeks of vacation. Might as well use a week or so. We're not at a critical point in the project."

"So, you've been planning to ask me for a while?"

"No, it came to me just now. I want to do this, Billy. We need to do this. It'll be our anniversary gift, okay? I feel like we're at a critical point here, you and me. I know you think I'm overreacting, as always. But I'm not. I want to be new to you. I want to . . . Oh," I said, seeing him unmoved, his eyes unfocused. "You think this is a bad idea. You had other plans."

"No, no. I'm just a little surprised. Really, Rennie. But no, it's a fine idea." he said. He set his coffee down lightly on the table. "Just great," he said.

I sat with my waffles and scrambled eggs, an impossibly cheerful yellow, and watched his smile tightening. But it could have been a trick of the light, the way the steam curled over his coffee mug, obscuring his expression. I couldn't tell for sure.

I stood at the edge of Hale Hina, straining to hear the forest. Although I couldn't quite make it out, I knew the valley lay in that deeper pool of shadow. A leap forward and I could fall into all that quiet.

"House of Hina so quiet you can hear roots of plants pushing deep, vines stretching," Apo Gina had once said, speaking in the local dialect—flattening out moist vowels, her tongue rolling fast over the sounds of *r*s and *g*s, the endings of words soft and limp.

"If you stay quiet long enough, you can hear the gods whispering secrets. Rennie, are you listening? All kinds of quiet on Lana'i. Which one means grief? Love? Which one always means bitterness?"

I had no answers. I was twelve years old.

"I don't know," I said, shrugging, not wishing to offend my aunt with the wild black hair shot through with silver.

Gently. That's how my cousins talked about Apo Gina and other relatives crazy or dead.

"Yes, you know. You run up Hale Hina how many times?" she demanded, her eyes sharp, missing nothing. "Use your ears next time."

I never knew whether to believe Apo Gina about the plants in the forest or the way people lied to each other and to themselves. But she had always shown me great kindness and that became a good enough reason for me to trust her. After my mother died and my father disappeared, becoming unrecognizable to me, his grief the only thing that sustained him over the years, Apo Gina moved in with us, becoming the only parent I could remember without feeling lost.

Before I left for college, when the demand for hexes and counter-hexes was still strong on the island, Apo Gina was regarded as a witch. People claimed she had a cure for everything: stomachaches, bad luck, malaise, sorrow. She knew all the herbs and roots and plants on the island and taught me everything she knew.

But her teachings on poisonous plants or aphrodisiacs—what could cure fatigue or heartache, what would calm a mild case of hives—was nothing compared to the history lesson of hands and faces and feet. I learned how to read the meaning of hands—how they can hold a body without loving it, how they can betray a voice—and feet: the import of clasped hands and feet crossed at the ankles, and how a man who is cheating on his wife will stand with his hips and feet wide apart as though he is waiting for the world to come to him. She taught me that there was no such thing as secrets because the human face, the body always gives itself away.

She also taught me the four kinds of liars, all of whom I could find on our island. I learned about pathological liars, those who cannot help themselves, their lies spilling over like flattery. Mr. Silva, he's like this, she said. Always smiling. Harmless.

The other kind of liar lies to get something.

They have no soul, Apo Gina said. They prey on the weak or the lonely. And the greedy. There is always the greedy, and most people are each of these things, some time or other, she said. Tricky to hold these liars. Holding them is like trying to sweep feathers into a dustpan. Hard to do, you see?

Then there are liars who run away from their lies. They lie to change their lives. They become somebody new because their old lives become too heavy. Do you understand, Rennie? We knew only of Susan McNeal, a transient who had the small, pinched face and the bottomless eyes of an alcoholic. She lived in a tent on the beach. In another life, she had had a family, a job, love.

But the worst kind of liars? The ones who lie to themselves, Apo Gina said. These people see things and keep quiet. Hear things; keep quiet. These are the most pitiful. You see? They know the truth but keep lying because is too hard to change, too much to lose, they think. Stuck in a bad habit. They hold on to one thing.

They think everything else is worth losing for this one thing. So weak, she said.

Which one are you, Rennie? she asked. I stared dumbly at her, startled at such a question. When it comes to your sister, you lie to yourself. Why?

I never answered. What Apo Gina would never understand was how much I loved Isabella, that I would have lied and cheated for her if she had asked me to. I knew this at nine. I felt I would always feel this. There was nothing Isabella could do that I couldn't forgive. She was the only family I had left, besides Apo Gina, and she was only a grandaunt. We were almost a generation apart.

Love is just a bad habit, Isabella agreed. Her comment seemed irrelevant, a nonsequitur.

I thought about this now as I sat on the ridge. I wanted to surrender to the deep stillness. Apo Gina was right—the gods at Hale Hina knew all my secrets. I threw a rock into the valley, scrambled down the ridge, and ran to Apo Gina's without looking back.

The smell of dried plants, of rich earth and time-blackened flowers, hung in the air when I opened the door to Apo Gina's workroom.

Awa root, pandanus leaves, and dried skins of eels dangled from plant hooks along one corner, opposite a bank of windows squinting from the August sun, but she kept most of her spells—dried, crushed, powdery, loose—in guava jelly jars and plastic bags on a four-tiered staggered bookshelf that she had made herself long ago. Apo Gina had wanted something sturdy to hold her sorcery in one place. It squatted along an entire wall, gap-toothed and brooding, most of the jars half empty: Apo Gina no longer practiced magic.

"Oh, sometimes I do, when people ask me," she said. "Sometimes your Aunt Elaine visits, she can't sleep, so I fix her something, or Mrs. Kimura wants something for her rash. But most people on the island, they say I'm just a crazy witch, using good-for-nothing tricks. I hear the gossip: *lolo, lolo, Apo Gina gettin' soft in da head now.* They say my magic is old and tired—my noni, awa, and mamaki is good only for making tea. But I know what I know. How easy for them to laugh, call me crazy. You still believe in my magic, Rennie?"

"Yes," I said simply, because there was nothing else I could say. I watched her face opening up. "I hope you don't let them get to you, Apo Gina."

"All their talking is no matter to me, Rennie," she clucked, stroking my hand as I tried to reassure her.

We sat in her kitchen, which joined her workroom at the shoulder and extended into her garden, walled in by a hibiscus hedge.

"How long you visiting?" she asked, my hands still in hers.

"About three days. Billy could only manage three days. He's in between these conferences. He's presenting a paper."

"Billy likes to have a big audience. I see your sister's visiting too. Same time as you."

"Yes, Isabella's here. A wild but nice coincidence."

"I'm not so sure is coincidence. No such thing as coincidence with your sister. You know this."

"No really, it was a fluke. Bella had no idea I'd be coming along.

Turns out she had been planning a trip home for a while. I miss her; I haven't seen her in weeks even though we live in the same city. You'd think we'd get together more often. She's never been one to return phone calls and she hasn't stopped by after her runs with Billy lately. It'll be good to see her."

"She and Billy—?"

"Yes. They're training for next year's marathon."

I felt an unbearable sadness, but felt compelled to continue talking. "Billy's shooting for a 3:30. Bella is trying to talk him into running it even faster, and Bella, as you know, can talk you into anything. Billy will probably go for it because that's the kind of guy he is and Apo Gina, I'm not sure, but—"

"Why you talking so fast? Slow down. Your face is red. What's wrong, Rennie? Here, drink this. Isabella and King and Billy coming over for breakfast?" She walked over to her stove to turn over the last batch of malasadas. "You and Isabella were never close. This is no surprise to me that you don't stay in touch."

"No, we've always been pretty close," I said, taking small sips of the bitter tea. "There was a bad time between us for a while, you know, after Mom died and during high school. What is this, Apo Gina?"

"Tea—for blurry vision."

"I can see just fine, Apo Gina."

"You have a bad habit, Rennie. You see everything, but you cover your eyes and your ears. I think maybe you like the dark."

"That's not true, Apo."

"All true. You don't admit. You make all kinds excuses for her.

Remember when you had warts all over your hands?"

How could I forget it? It was the summer I was ten, the summer warts sprouted all over my fingers, a ring of gray cauliflowerlike blooms along the cuticles. I don't remember how I got them in the first place—who knows how these things happen?—but I do remember that after two weeks of hiding my hands in the folds of my muumuus, and rubbing the bumpy growths as if I could wear them away if I rubbed long enough, I became desperate to get rid of them. I found a razor blade in my father's razor and shaved off the top layer of one of the warts. I watched spellbound as blood spurted from the severed head, surprised at the sting of pain. I never expected these warm, bristly nubs were part of my own skin.

By the time I went to Apo Gina for help, the warts had spread to the insides of my fingers.

She took my hands and ran her fingers along the budding heads. She didn't look away in disgust as Isabella had.

We need kukui oil, was all she said as she examined my fingers thoughtfully, turning them over and over, as though she was studying a geography of my hands, a language I was too young to learn. Her knuckles were wide and deeply whorled. My hands in hers felt meaningful.

She wrapped my fingers in a rough cloth damp with brown kukui oil and instructed me to apply the oil for two weeks before bedtime. "For two weeks, don't look at your hands, Rennie," she said. "Can you do this?"

I imagined running with my hands clenched, unnatural to me,

but I told her I would try. "No," she insisted, "no trying. Do it. You must believe they will be *ma-mio,* disappeared. You must already see it."

"Yes," I said and I imagined my hands were already smooth and brown. I imagined the astonishment of the girls in my hula dance class who cringed and backed away from me during dance drills. They whispered that I had ma'i pake, and that I should join the rest of the cursed on Molokai's windswept coast.

"It's not leprosy!" I shouted one day, giving a name to their whispers. "Isabella, tell them it's not leprosy."

Everyone turned to look at Isabella, who stood at the end of the small dance floor. But she only shrugged her shoulders, shifted her hips as though she might do the ueki, and looked at the wall in front of her. Her right foot rubbed her left toe.

"I didn't hear you, Rennie. Honest. And even if I had, but I hadn't, how would saying there were warts have helped?" Isabella retorted, two body lengths ahead of me as we walked home. "It wouldn't have. Trust me. Warts are warts are gross. You're becoming a witch, Rennie!"

"You could've said something, Bella," I said, trying not to cry, catching up her. "Anything. You could've said anything. They would've believed you."

"Yeah . . . well. Maybe I should've. If I'd heard you, I mean. But they're right, Rennie, do you know how disgusting they are? They do look like leprosy."

"Do you see this," I imagined saying to the dance class as my hands swept and caressed the air recalling valleys and oceans in perfect time to Pu'u o' Manoa. "My Apo Gina has performed a miracle. I am myself again."

I imagined Isabella leading the circle in applause. "My sister, Renata Marie, is no longer lepolepo," I imagined Isabella saying, "the curse has been lifted."

Apo Gina would tell me later that kukui oil was nothing more than candlenut oil and faith alone made my warts disappear.

"I guess there's something to Apo Gina's voodoo after all," Isabella sniffed when I showed her my hands. "Are you going to be her little apprentice now? You know Mom thought she was crazy."

It was that moment that I realized something about Isabella, an understanding that knocked the wind out of me. I felt my mind open up to hold the thought and understood that it was submerged and I could only see the luminous tip of it. The truth was this—she was one of those people who lived life weightless, that she had no center of gravity, nothing that would hold her down, or compel her to stay; there was no one and nothing in her life that would cause her sorrow. She would live with her hands open, fingers trailing space, skimming the skin, just staying long enough in a room, in a life, to remain unforgettable. She would leave them, leave me, aching. She would make no exceptions.

I drank the last of Apo Gina's tea.

"Are you seeing now, Rennie? What did you hear at Hale Hina? Why you run there this morning? You see this? You already know."

"What are you talking about? I don't know what you mean!" I

said, but my voice fractured like brittle glass. Apo Gina held my hands, then my face.

"You know your sister, Rennie. She cannot hold you or me. Not strong enough, you see. She thinks by taking and keeping to herself she becomes strong, so her whole life she is selfish. But Isabella, she stays small. She cannot give. She don't know how." Her voice fell and I understood that like me, Apo Gina had tried for years to enter Bella's heart.

Something broke inside me. "I've known for so long, Apo Gina. I don't know how and I didn't trust it, and I didn't want to know because she's my sister. She's my sister."

"She's your sister," Apo Gina repeated, "and you can live with this?" I turned to face her and realized how I much I loved her, and that I had never told her what she meant to me. There were silences, even with those I understood and who loved me in return. Before I could answer her, Billy and King and Isabella arrived.

Isabella hugged me tightly. "I've missed you," she said with such sweetness that I felt disarmed.

"I ran up to Hale Hina this morning," I heard myself say. "Watched the sun come up. You would have loved it, Bella."

I couldn't hear what she said to me. I saw only her smile, Billy's smile, King's. Images of breakfast blurred and slowed and I felt myself floating curiously above Apo Gina's hardwood floors. I did not feel like myself. "What's in this tea, Apo?"

I saw Billy's face, inscrutable as a loaf of bread. He mumbled something about running to the beach. "Really? I was sure you were with Bella this morning," I heard myself say, "running, I mean." And I watched relief wash over his face when I said this.

Billy sat next to Isabella. King was on her right. Apo Gina swirled in slow circles, pouring coffee, pouring juice, her muumuu grazing the floor. She reached for my hand and held it. My hand fit easily in hers and the swirly feeling disappeared. Apo Gina's breakfast nook righted itself, falling with a thud it seemed, the light in the room pale and narrow.

They had the sweet flush of lovers: my husband and my sister. I had known about them after their first long run together, when they had arrived breathless, giddy, and I had turned to look the other way.

I watched Isabella watching Apo Gina, her arm next to Billy's on the table. Her right hand traced the graceful line of her chin, down to her neck, and rested in the pale dip of her collarbone. King shoved malasadas and forkfuls of eggs into his mouth. I wondered if he knew or if he always ate with such gusto in the face of his wife's betrayal.

After breakfast, after everyone cleared the table and Apo Gina took Billy and King out to her garden, I sat with my sister at the table, feeling like myself again. She had the drowsy look of overindulgence.

"That was some breakfast! That woman can cook. The island air always gets me hungry," she said.

"Yes, Apo Gina is extraordinary. Rare, really. You've always had a big appetite, Bella. Huge," I said. "Amazing. How do you do it?"

A shadow creased her lovely face. "How do I do what?"

"How long has it been going on, Bella?"

"What? What are you talking about?"

"Don't," I said evenly. "Don't insult me."

"Okay," she said slowly, as if feeling her way to me. "But it's over." She pulled and rubbed the lobe of her right ear: the nervous tics of liars. "We agreed to end it after this trip. It's over."

She blinked once and held her gaze.

"You're lying," I said, hearing her feet rustle under the table. "Your feet are nervous. You're scratching your left toe with your right. You're swallowing hard." Her face grew still.

"I don't know what you're talking about," she said.

"I don't know who you are, Bella. And I don't think you've ever known me. After mom died, I thought you were all I had left, and I used to feel so awful that I'd never get to know you. All I wanted was to be close to you, the way we were at the top of Hale Hina all those mornings. I kept hoping we'd go back there, just you and me. I wanted to believe that you had felt that too, that I hadn't imagined it, that it had been real. But I realize now I was just missing mom all those years. That ache wasn't for you. I've wasted so much time believing you were worth getting to know."

"Rennie," she sobbed. I heard her rambling about how she would end it, that she was so so sorry, that she and Billy never meant for this to happen. I imagined her mouth opening and closing, drawing in air, her hands gesturing wildly.

I had spoken a truth, and there it was, undeniable and unflinching. I kept my eyes on the floor, afraid that if I looked at my sister she might be *ma-mio,* might disappear before me. Dry leaves scuttled across Apo Gina's patio. Isabella and I sat mutely for what seemed like hours. But it could have been only a matter of minutes.

I heard the sound of my sister's breathing, broken, labored, I felt her hand rest on my shoulder and felt her finger tracing letters on my back.

R-E-N-N-I-E, R-E-N-N-I-E, she spelled over and over: an incantation.

I think I read my name, but her finger was racing so fast along my back, her hand gripping my shoulder as if she were falling, her fingers swooping like a bird, alighting, clawing the air, soaring so fast that I couldn't quite read it. I couldn't be sure.

Nelinia Cabiles has been running for over fifteen years—since she was thirteen years old—and has run everything from 5Ks to marathons. She would eventually like to run an ultramarathon.

Char Simons

Birthing a Running Family

Rhythmic drumming of rain on the roof sounds the day's alarm. The trenchcoat-colored light brings little heat to the winter air. I pull the covers closer around me.

Already wedged together like three spoons in a silverware drawer, I draw the two sleeping little bodies closer. Hugging the mattress on the other side of the bed lies my husband, Jeff, with his own spoons—our two beagles, Homer and Fairbanks.

The warmth of our sons' bodies wrapped with mine, coupled with contented sighs when I hug them, are too much.

I will run later in the day, for sure. But the race can wait.

Life hadn't always been like this. Throughout five pregnancies in four years, three miscarriages and two births, I remained a fiercely competitive, if middle-of-the-pack, runner and triathlete. Breastfeeding, poopy diapers, sleep deprivation, and a part-time job were no obstacles.

I'd train six days a week and race monthly, reveling in the luxurious expanse of time when I could focus on doing just one task, rather than six simultaneously. Racing and training were my quiet time.

The day following my monthly race ritual, I'd put Taylor in a stroller, Mackey in a backpack, and take them to the park or on a hike. Sometimes I'd strap both of them into the bike trailer for a ride through the forested, rolling countryside. When the weather was bad, we went to the children's museum or swimming at the Y. Either way, I got to spend the day with the boys and Jeff got a break.

And so went the familial rhythm for the first four years of Taylor's life, and the first two of Mackey's.

So what is happening? Does bagging the traditional New Year's Day five-mile Resolution Run—the one I had so proudly waddled through at two months postpartum—mean I am going soft? What next? Skipping a workout because the boys had runny noses? Forsaking the friends, vitality, and peace of mind that come from aerobic playtime? Would I abandon me? Who would I become?

The drumbeat of the rain continues. I pull the down comforter and the boys closer still, and ease back into sleep. The answers to those questions, like the race, can wait.

The thought of not working out during pregnancy and after childbirth never occurred to me. For twenty years, I ran, swam, sweated, and bicycled, competing in dozens of running races and triathlons and crisscrossing Europe and the United States by bicycle. Extremes of weather in the Midwest, where I grew up, and the mores of the Mediterranean, where I lived for part of my 20s, were no deterrents.

In Indiana, adapting sometimes meant waiting out a blizzard.

One day while in college, the snow whirled and swirled throughout the stark December day. Looking out the window from my tenth floor dorm room, I waited and wondered. Run now? Run later? Not run at all? Shortly after dark, the snow stopped, the heavens parted, and a bitter seven-degree chill set in. It was a beautiful night for a run through the hilly campus.

In densely packed Italy, adjusting sport to culture meant beating the morning traffic. I would rise as soon as the metal *serratura* screeched below my second-floor apartment window, signaling that Mario's Espresso Bar was open for business. Only at that early morning hour were the streets of Milan quiet enough to run to the small, green haven of Giardini Pubblici.

Given those conditions, what was a little pregnancy in terms of training? My own pregnancy game plan, designed to keep baby safe and Mom sane, was simple: no racing and no track workouts. Also, no bicycling, at least not after the second month of pregnancy, when breathing and simultaneously bending over the drops became impossible.

One of the joys of working out for decades is that the body signals—subtly, yet unmistakably—when it's changing. One late-May day, when strong shafts of golden sunlight lingered in the sky until late evening and the air smelled of the fragrance of blooming rhododendrons, my belly had just a hint of bloat. The evening before, Jeff and I had feasted on mountains of homemade hummus, salad, pasta, wine, and pie. A protruding tummy after a homemade dinner with friends was pretty standard, but by the next morning my innards were usually back to normal.

Not this time. An overdue period a few days later, followed by a pregnancy test confirmed what my body had already put me on notice for: a zygote!

Along with the usual fanfare of an impending first baby, my pregnancy workout plan took effect. That the baby was due on leap day was fitting. Except for slight, periodic morning sickness and sluggishness, I felt fine. Jeff and I spent the Fourth of July weekend camping in the arid highlands near Bend, Oregon. A country-mile run one morning turned out to be more like seven, but I took it slow and drank lots of water afterward.

The drive back to Olympia at the end of the weekend was long and hot. As soon as Jeff stopped the car in front of our house, I jumped out and ran to the bathroom as is customary—pregnant or not—after a five-hour car trip. The blood that flowed out, however, was anything but customary.

I knew nothing about miscarriages, nor did I know anyone who had had one—I thought. After three, though, I would learn a lot about them. More blood and an ultrasound showing the gray shadings of an empty sac confirmed what my body had blared so plainly: that the tiny being whom I'd barely begun to know and love was gone.

As Jeff and I tried to figure out how, or if, to grieve, friends came out of the woodwork with miscarriage stories of their own—Joan lost half a set of twins, Helena miscarried twice, Steve's mom had six. All had gone on to have more than one child. I would too, they assured.

Healing the body from loss was easier than healing the heart. Instinctively, I developed a postmiscarriage ritual, some type of physical challenge. Competing as best I could only two weeks post-miscarriage, the Run from the Bears 10K served as a purifier, a physical cleansing, as if sweat could wash away the pain.

Like the first, the second miscarriage came at about twelve weeks after conception. The pregnancy had seemed quite uneventful—until the bleeding started. Whereas I'd passed the first fetus at home, the second time I was convinced to have a D & C. While in the clinic waiting to have the procedure, I went to the bathroom and, in a burst of pain and blood, passed the fetal sac.

While the first miscarriage could be chalked up to a freak incident or bad luck, the second one left me shaken and doubtful of ever bearing a child. My body had betrayed me once again. This time, a mere 10K wouldn't cut it for the postmiscarriage athletic event. Stronger anesthetic was needed. Like RAMROD—Ride Around Mount Rainier in One Day.

The twelve-and-a-half-hour, 156-mile event was a physical victory—never had I cycled so far in one day. The six weeks of training were just as healing as the ride itself. I have found peace and solace in mountains ever since age three when I spent my first summer at my grandmother's in Switzerland. That I now live within sight of Mount Rainier is nothing short of divine planning. Training for RAMROD meant that on weekends, I would toss my Schwinn LeTour into the back of the Honda Civic and drive to the mountains for a day of cycling. Either alone or with friends, I would circle parts of the mountain while my soul—and the souls of the two little beings I had lost—soared together among the rugged cliffs and gleaming glaciers.

By the time the third pregnancy rolled around, I was prepared for another miscarriage. Jeff and I had begun adoption proceedings. At twelve weeks, I had an ultrasound. Usually not done until mid-pregnancy, our doctor agreed to an early one to ease our fears —or confirm our nightmares. Even at this early stage, if the fetus were still alive and developing, Dr. Gage would be able to tell.

With Jeff holding my hand, tightly, I lay on the exam table. Unable to look at the monitor, I focused on the blank wall as the vaginal wand searched for life.

"There's the heartbeat!" Dr. Gage exclaimed.

Jeff and I cried with relief. We had come farther in this pregnancy than ever before. The first precarious trimester was over. We were finally going to have a baby! Although we still had six months to go before birth, caution and fear of miscarriage left me. Little Taylor would be all right.

Having given up racing, biking, and track intervals the first trimester, the athletic challenge shifted to how much and how much longer. How long into pregnancy would I be able to swim and run? How much would I be able to do? How much would I want to do?

In the second trimester, I dropped my running mileage by five miles a week. During the final three months, I would drop it five more. Swimming would stay fairly steady. Besides, summer had finally arrived—in August—which meant lake season. Symmetrical Ward Lake was about a mile around and two-thirds of a mile across and back. Ringed by cedars, Douglas fir and a few houses, the brisk, seventy-degree lake lent itself to short swims during the late summer that lingered into October. That I could no longer squeeze into a wet suit also made shorter but more frequent swims appealing.

Entering the third trimester, running became more difficult. With every step, Taylor bounced on my bladder. Although I habitually vary running routes for a change of scenery, the necessity of pit stops was thrown into the planning. Convenience stores with friendly clerks, gas stations, fast-food joints, or, at the very least, woods had to be part of the course. In multiples. The Capitol Lake loop, with mile splits marked by a Jack in the Box, two public rest rooms and a Sani-can at a school ball field worked well. Less amenable was another favorite four-mile loop through neatly landscaped neighborhoods serviced only by a fire station and a clump of forest.

Despite numerous bathroom stops, running any distance at all was becoming increasingly uncomfortable. But I was on a mission —to trot to the hospital when the time came and deliver this baby. Never mind the cranky clerk at the Frog Pond Grocery who, when I stopped during a workout to use the bathroom, told me I shouldn't be running anyway.

One hot, sunny August day at seven and a half months pregnant, I was about halfway into that four-mile, bathroom-scarce loop when something snapped. I not only felt it, I heard it, the sound coming from my backside. Adhering to running custom, I ignored the pain and hobbled home.

For several days, I could only lie on the couch and moan. Even walking hurt. Taylor, however, was fine, even a little more spirited than usual. A lively fetus, especially at bedtime when my stomach undulated with his gyrations, he seemed to miss the rhythm of running that had rocked him to sleep since conception.

The chiropractor said, basically, that I had pulled a muscle in my butt, which had thrown my back out of alignment. He put me back together again, but suggested no physical activity other than walking.

I ignored his advice and continued swimming. Water felt luxurious. Only in such an embryonic world did I feel light. On Taylor's due date, I swam two thousand yards, including two hundred butterfly.

They say an easy pregnancy means a hard birth. I should have known. After two days of labor kicked off by bad chicken livers and food poisoning, Taylor emerged via cesarean section. With dark hair, olive skin, and almond-shaped eyes that reflected his Japanese heritage, the eight-pound, four-ounce tyke was dubbed the little barracuda for wiggling up to my nipple to suck the moment we touched one another.

A C-section meant no swimming for a month, no running for six weeks. With Taylor born in late October, my race debut would be the Anderson Island run the week before Christmas. Islands in the Puget Sound are anything but flat, yet this race is my perennial favorite. Only this year, I would be huffing through the 2.6-mile course rather than the 9.6-mile route I usually tackled. Father and son would stay home, so a breast pump came along with the Adidas.

Feeling jello-y and jiggly, I nonetheless ran eight-minute miles. A victory, for this time I got to reclaim my body out of triumph, not defeat.

Ten years earlier, I had completed my first and only marathon, curious to experience what all the fuss was about. Despite a respectable 3:40 finish, one marathon was enough. Until age and time played tricks on my mind.

"I wonder how it would feel to do another one," I said to Jeff in the afterglow of Anderson Island.

"Why don't you join the marathon training group and do Capital City this spring?" he suggested.

So at two months postpartum, I tested the waters with an eight-mile run. I almost phoned Jeff at mile six for a ride home when I thought my uterus was going to fall out. Nonetheless, I joined the training group, determined to find the answer to that burning question: Would the last 10K of a marathon hurt as much as they did the first time?

Training proceeded uneventfully except for popping painkillers before a long run and soaking my sore belly in hot bathwater afterward. My goal of a marathon reprise, however, halted abruptly the week before the race. My beloved Grossmuetti had died in Switzerland at age ninety-two—three weeks before she was to meet her first great-grandchild for the first time. I flew with seven-month-old Taylor to her funeral.

Back home after the funeral, summer race season was in full swing. The 30–39 age category is the toughest in women's running and triathlon and littered with seasoned champions. Some are childless with lots of time, money, and energy for training. Others, like Sarah Graham, one of the Pacific Northwest's top amateur triathletes, squeeze in training between changing diapers and packing preschool lunches. Seeing another mom at races crowned women's champion helped reassure me that it was okay to hang on to the athletic part of me despite motherhood.

Always on the lookout for new racing venues, I decided to try the Great Columbia Crossing in the fall. The Columbia near its mouth is a notorious wind tunnel, making for world-renowned windsurfing but dubious running. I was prepared to get friendly with the bridge guardrail.

Instead, race day was sunny, calm, and hot. Northwesterners complain when the temperature rises above seventy, which I always thought was kind of wimpy. But on this day, the heat zapped me.

After three pregnancies, I didn't need a drugstore kit to tell me I was with child. Yet Jeff insisted on getting one. A drop of urine into the plastic well, a thirty-second wait, and a red + confirmed that Taylor was going to have a sibling.

I'm an only child, a title I never relished. After summer evenings of playing kick-the-can with neighborhood kids, they would go home in twos and threes, to continue playing. I went home alone. Jeff, on the other hand, was the youngest of three. Although the total number was undecided, Jeff and I had always planned to have more than one child. But this little one was not to be either, its soul taking flight just before Christmas.

Five weeks after the third miscarriage, Jeff and I again conceived. I would have preferred not to know about this latest one until after the precarious first trimester was over. I tried to forget about the being inside me so as not to be stabbed by disappointment again when the bleeding started.

And the bleeding did start.

"It's happening again!" I sobbed, pacing around the living room trying to figure out what to do next.

Angry, fearful, and shaking, I ran out the door. A four-mile run would neither kill nor rescue any fetus that was on its way out. Afterward, I called Jeff and Dr. Gage. We did an ultrasound, but the results were inconclusive. We would have to wait ten days for another one.

No marathon, no triathlon, no coast-to-coast bike trip took as long as those ten days between ultrasounds. I had already given up hope, and called the adoption agency to reinstate our application. I also did my ritual postmiscarriage athletic event, this time a 10k race along the Wishkah River in Aberdeen.

The day was hot, dry, and sunny, the course was flat—my least favorite running conditions. The race felt hard and I struggled across the finish line in just over forty-eight minutes. A few days later, the ultrasound proved Mackey was miraculously still with us. Mackey was a fighter.

Not wanting this pregnancy to be an athletic pain in the butt like Taylor's was, I early on consented to give up running at the end of six months. Actually, it was a relief. Running into the final stages of pregnancy, belly swaying, had been merely a test of will. I'd proven I could do it, and I didn't need to do it again. I'd continue swimming, and also treat myself to a three-day mountain hike with women friends to kick off the last trimester and the start of my running hiatus.

With Taylor, there had been days of premature labor before the real thing set in. With Mackey, all was silent, so I figured he'd be about a week late. Not so. Labor started with all the swiftness of a starter's gun. I barely had time to pack, shower, and wake up Jeff before going to the hospital.

Runners' vaginal muscles are often so well developed that they become rigid and somewhat useless for pushing a baby out during labor. Nonetheless, I wanted to give a vaginal delivery a shot, feeling somewhat cheated from the drugged experience of Taylor's birth.

Once at the hospital, contractions came at a fever pitch. When I pushed, Jeff, standing at the foot of the bed, could see a dark mop of hair emerging from my vagina. When I stopped pushing, the head would recede into the womb. After a couple of hours of seesawing, doctor and patient agreed to surrender to the knife and another C-section. Mackey emerged a healthy eight pounds, with the same black hair and dark eyes as big brother.

A few weeks later, I resumed training. But no longer at 5 A.M. A second child had done me in, in terms of morning exercise. Swimming, running, and, later, bike workouts shifted to afternoon. Two years of sleep deprivation had caught up with me.

If parents are more relaxed with a second child, the same can be said about getting back in shape. I was much more laid back about conquering athletic heights. No marathon training this time around. Rather, my athletic goal for the year was a modest ten-miler as part of a relay team running between Jasper and Banff on an awesome ribbon of highway that winds through the Canadian Rockies and past great horned sheep and an occasional grizzly bear. I was going for scenery rather than struggle this year.

Aside from the hot, uphill leg of Jasper-Banff, the biggest challenge of the trip were my breasts. Slipping to the back of a van full of mostly men, I subtly tried to whip out the breast pump. While the first session was met with an uncomfortable silence, by the end of the trip, cow jokes were flying.

The breast-feeding issue, however, symbolized a deeper dilemma: the struggle to balance the new mom and the old me. Swelled to the point of leakage every couple of hours at the beginning of the five-day trip, by the end my breast milk was down to a few hard-pumped droplets. My milk was drying up, and I wondered if even the splendor of the Canadian Rockies was worth it.

Leaving immediately after the race, I pumped, prayed, and cried all the way home. At almost eight months, Mackey was increasingly interested in strained beets and spinach anyway. But I hoped he would still enjoy a nip from Mom now and then, at least for a little while longer. He did, but soon Mom and babe were both weaned.

The pinnacle of competition over for the year, I settled into an enjoyable, if nondescript, running and triathlon season. Jasper-Banff, though, had made travel the athletic theme of the year. So when my friend Kate asked me to provide moral support for her at the Victoria Marathon, there was no question. I'd go, run the accompanying 8K, and relish watching marathoners cross the finish line.

The weekend in Victoria, British Columbia, was memorable in many respects—cheering on Kate and greeting her at the finish line with flowers, hearing marathon legend Bill Rodgers speak at a symposium, and inhaling a pre-race buffet that wouldn't end. The highlight, however, was a modest brochure I happened upon at packet pickup and tucked away for contemplation: the Victoria Half Ironman Triathlon, eight months away.

A half Ironman represented the great unknown. Could I go more than twice as far as I'd ever gone in a triathlon?

Weekends were the highlight of the training season. A flexible, unflappable, and long-suffering husband gave me the luxury of time necessary for long workouts. For up to five hours, Jeff took care of two testosterone-driven toddlers while I swam, biked and ran to oblivion. It was no contest who had the harder job. I came home from workouts refreshed. Jeff ended his marathon babysitting sessions looking haggard and in need of a nap.

For four months, I ate, slept, and breathed triathlon. When I wasn't training—which wasn't often —I was thinking about it. Visualization is a crucial, though often overlooked, component of competition. With sleek strokes, rapid cadence, and a steady stride, I would cruise through Victoria with Jeff and the boys waiting at the finish line. The biggest mental hurdles were cold lake water and competing early in the morning after what was sure to be another night of sleep interrupted by "Juice, juice!" and "Momma, I need a new dyedee."

Race day dawned cool and cloudy—perfect conditions. My goals were modest: to finish and to feel no pain. If all went well, I would come in at about six hours, forty minutes.

And the race did go well. There was never a point in the swim —despite backstroking for a while to get into a breathing rhythm —when I thought 'this hurts too much to go on.' There was never a time during the three-loop bike course when I didn't enjoy the view of rolling hills dotted with neat, English-style houses and farms. There was never a moment during the two-loop run, despite diarrhea, that I didn't enjoy the soft, shady trail and watching picnickers revel in the lake and along the sandy beaches. Although finish-line pictures showed a haggard, weary woman with bags the size of Toledo under her eyes, it would be a good week before the adrenaline of the race dissipated and I felt truly tired.

So in six short months, how did I get from triumphant half ironwoman to dropping out of a race before it even started?

Somewhere along the way, Taylor and Mackey became people and I became a mom. Odds are, triathlons and running—the latter of which has been around for a few millennia—are going to be here for a while longer. Meanwhile, our sons will only be with us for a few short years, years that are going by quicker than Mackey can spill his milk.

The intensity of racing, training, and lofty athletic goals served their purpose. In the process, I'd reached heights I might not have been tempted to try without children. I'd planted the seed in our kids that the dance of motion can be a lifelong joy, and I get a charge when the boys don sneakers to jog around the block with me or I overhear Taylor tell his buddies that his mom's a runner.

My athletic goal for this year is a bit different. It's to take the boys camping once a month, athletic events to be sure. Yet even as racing was becoming a rapidly fading memory, the application for Dugan's Run arrived in the mail. Last year, Taylor placed second in the toddler race and I won free go-cart passes at the postrace raffle. Nonetheless, I was about to toss this year's application into the recycle box when Jeff caught a glimpse of it.

"Are you gonna do it this year?" he asked.

"Nah. I don't feel like hurting."

"Oh, come on. Why don't you do it? We could make it a family thing. Spudie could do the kids' race again, and Doodle's old enough this year to do it too. Besides, they have great pizza afterward," Jeff urged.

Ocean Shores, three weeks later. We clean up at the awards ceremony. Taylor and Mackey sweep the boys' four-and-under division with one-two finishes. I come in a second in the women's 35–44. After lunch, we toss our shoes aside and let the rollicking waves chase us on the expansive, sandy beach. Racing was no longer my quiet time. It had become something much, much better.

Mary Kinnunen

Pikku Lintu

What are you, some kind of feminist?"

"Look—all I'm saying is, why can't we just let them race as athletes instead of boys and girls?"

This Finnish granny with arched eyebrows and a thick accent bore down on me as our offspring hustled mightily toward the finish line in the FinnFest '94 Youth Road Race. Then she turned away with a "Humph!"

I thought this antagonistic behavior unusual for the usually reserved Finns, the tribe that *60 Minutes* tagged, the Shyest People in the World. I should know, I'm a third-generation *Amerikan Suomalainen.*

So why was I standing on Northern Illinois University's campus, during a cultural festival of all things, quibbling with a family from Nebraska?

The night before, my nine-year-old daughter Eleanor had noticed the race listed in the festival program, and had asked if she could enter. Sure. After two days of wall-to-wall concerts, lectures, demonstrations, baked goods, and coffee, a footrace in the open air sounded great.

The next morning, while my mother was delivering one of those lectures, Eleanor and I headed over to NIU's sports complex. The race official, decked out in a blue and white SUOMI running suit, explained that the one-kilometer course would take the runners around several buildings, ending at the finish line inside the gym.

The only kids who signed up to race were Eleanor and three boys: ten- and sixteen-year-old brothers, and a fourteen-year-old. When Eleanor showed up, a rather loud uncle, I believe, jabbed the ten-year-old. "Oh ho, a girl! Are you going to let *her* beat you?" he asked, then laughed. The boy smiled weakly.

Dressed in solid pink with baby blue Keds, Eleanor was four and a half feet of skin and bones. She didn't look like much of a challenge. In fact, one of her nicknames, which has stuck throughout the years is Pikku Lintu (pih-koo lihn-tu), which means "little bird" in Finnish.

Upon hearing the uncle's remark, Eleanor looked at me with the expression she gets when somebody asks her to "Say something in Chinese!" (My family spent a year in the People's Republic.)

A couple of years earlier, she'd been racing her bicycle in BMX and had crashed into the dusty track just as a man yelled out to his son, who was trailing Ellie, "Pedal! Don't let that *girl* beat you!" As I turned to say something to the father, the boy ran over her, cracking her collarbone. She healed just fine but hasn't wanted to race her bike since.

Now she once again found herself the wild card, the loose cannon, the ponytailed contention of XX chromosomes. And all she wanted to do was run and have some fun.

The mom confided to me that her boys had been practicing their starts and running all week. I didn't tell her Eleanor was doing this on a lark.

Somebody blew a whistle and off they went. We elders began to wait. The granny was fretting. The uncle was pacing. The mom had her Instamatic poised.

Finally, the sixteen-year-old appeared in the distance. A minute or so later came the ten-year-old with Eleanor two lengths behind. The fourteen-year-old was nowhere in sight. The small crowd squealed and I could feel my heart in my chest. Those kids were running hard, and August in corn country is hot.

The other family started to yell the boy's name, and I found myself adding "Eleanor!" to "Come on! Come on!"

The duo was twenty yards from the building's entrance when the pink shirt turned into a pink blur. The uncle yelled, "Whoa! Did you see that?" as the two runners sped into the gym neck and neck.

We walked inside to find our kids sucking air. I put an arm around Eleanor and squeezed her tight.

"Mom," she said, "you know that boy?"

"Yes."

"I beat him," she said quietly.

I grinned. "You mean ya smoked him!" I whispered back.

"I read about that somewhere—how you don't use up all your energy at the beginning."

My goodness, she had a plan.

The other mom came over and smiled graciously. "Look! She's

not even tired. You did very well." She offered to take Eleanor's picture since I didn't have a camera.

The coach walked by Eleanor, pointed at her, and said, "Good race."

"Thanks, thanks a lot, thank you."

The boy shuffled up and shook her hand, turning his head away.

The uncle exclaimed he'd never seen such an exciting finish. "Never!"

My mother could never bear to watch me play high school tennis, saying she always found herself wishing the matches could end in ties. But I'll be there for Eleanor, bringing my sweaty palms and cardiac palpitations with me. That day in DeKalb a young person discovered the athlete in herself.

Now she's a few inches taller and still has a ways to go to a hundred pounds. She's on the junior high cross-country team, and she's doing well at it. She's racing through zoos and bogs, over golf courses, around buildings and parking lots; she's having herself some fun. I'm glad I stuck up for her that day in DeKalb, and I still wait till the last runner is in before leaving the finish line. I applaud them through their pain. There are no ties in this, either.

Mary Kinnunen's poems and essays have appeared in a variety of publications. She is editor of Red, White & a Paler Shade of Blue—*poems on the Finnish American experience.* Hello Quality Control, *a chapbook of her poetry, was published in 1998. She lives in Rhinelander, Wisconsin, where she serves as alderperson on the city council.*

Isis Amelia Rose Sien

A Sense of Reason

It is said that a child develops a sense of reason at age seven. I wonder when it is that we lose this ability again. As a second-grader, I sat on the school jungle gym, for the first time left truly alone with my thoughts, and realized that my presence on Earth bore little significance. People loved me, but only because I was there. In the absence of my birth, that love would have been given to someone else. This realization was originally undisturbing, but later I worked desperately to prove myself wrong.

As the years progressed I strove to discover my evasive individual importance, thinking that some unknown action would magically validate my existence, not to others, but to myself, which is strange when I realized that I had already decided I was of little significance. These questions coincided with the starting gun beginning adolescence, leaving me vulnerable to the cruel predators middle schools cultivate. Suddenly, it became more important to blend in than to stand out. I sacrificed my individuality for a chance at popularity, just as the little mermaid exchanged her voice for feet, thus enabling her to marry her human prince. Though I am unsure of the results of the mermaid's exchange—marriage is, or should be, more permanent than junior high—I managed to keep my voice *and* my feet, in more ways than I ever would have imagined.

My search for acceptance with the jocks led me to make a klutzy attempt at a wide array of sports, eventually compelling me to run on my seventh-grade cross-country team. I was certainly no star—I stopped at least once a mile, even in meets—but it caught my attention. Running caused fatigue in parts of my body I didn't even know existed, yet I did it day after day, even after the cross-country season was over. Soon, I was serious about running, not because I was talented but because I was too obstinate to admit defeat.

By freshman year, running had become a passion, not a demon, and I had a wall of trophies and bib numbers to prove it. I have even gained the respect of the jocks, though it no longer matters so much; my high school is too big for one "in" group, and cross-country runners are the rebel athletes anyway. We choose tofu over hamburgers, political debates over cussing matches, and actually intend to go to college on academic merits. We have carved calculus equations into the track, engaged in chalk combat as we marked our home course, and taken more than a few kooky detours. Many of my teammates became friends, friends became teammates (it is a guaranteed way to see a lot of me), and I have developed a connection with everyone I run with.

My nonrunning friends (I am, after all, a tolerant person) have learned to accept my running-related eccentricities (actually, the rest of my eccentricities too), admiring my "sexy" running outfits; giving me hugs even when I'm coated in a thick, cloying sweat; and dressing in outrageous outfits to cheer me on during races. Others are not as understanding, like the men who leer from their cars as they pass me, forcing me to risk my safety and put up with it or relinquish my independence and always run with guys. There are also those like my school principal, who after reviewing cross-country recruiting posters that listed a variety of reasons to join the team told a friend and me that we only ran to get dates. If that was my primary goal, there are far simpler routes to a date than running forty miles a week! But even those who tolerate the strange habits of a runner question the logic of my ways.

While I readily admit that I'm a few standard deviations from the norm, I believe logic is irrational. In mathematics, it is taught that nothing is either logical or true until it is proven by a complex series of conjectures, theorems, and postulates. Yet these "laws" used to build the foundation for logic are simply "assumed to be true" without further explanation or exploration. While these rules appear sensible, these same teachings mandate that *nothing* can be assumed. Thus, it is not crushing when I am informed that running is illogical.

My freshman year in high school was a culmination of the anger and sorrow that had been repressed for years, held back because of the societal message that women must be caregivers, sacrificing our needs to help those around us. I obeyed, holding together not only my life, but that of an emotionally dependent friend. In the same way that I had always channeled my emotion into schoolwork, my running now also flourished, transforming emotional compost into a high-mileage, fast-time garden. As my emotional numbness faded, I began to see the interconnection of my physical and emotional states. Though an onslaught of injuries created unhappy withdrawals from running, they allowed me to recognize my emotions, a skill that, along with reason, had been left behind, lost, or perhaps abandoned. Within eight months, I whiplashed my neck, reminding me to pay attention to my head, especially my mind; I conquered anemia, refusing to be weak; I sprained my lower back, an alert that I could not carry anyone else's burdens until I had dealt with my own, probably an eternal battle; and a stress fracture showed me the divisive choices I had to face.

As I approach my sixteenth birthday, I run hard, run to get faster. I have a strong support team, but in the end I rely on myself, alone as I charge through a 5K, alone as I navigate the hills of a half marathon. Alone. Alone because I have the strength and motivation to get what I want. A sense of reason.

Isis Amelia Rose Sien was born and raised in Santa Cruz, California, and now attends the University of California at Berkeley. In addition to preparing for law school, she loves running, biking, traveling in Latin America, and spending time with her friends. She wrote "A Sense of Reason" when she was fifteen, while running varsity cross-country for Santa Cruz High School.

Dorothy L. Kangas

Looking Back

The sun was hot on my bare shoulders as I stretched to touch my toes. I was stiff from the previous day's run, and the sore muscles in my thighs begged to be stretched as I paced slowly around the starting line. I saw my mother in the distance, talking to one of the old ladies who had come to watch the race. She glanced in my direction and I waved, silently wishing I had stayed in bed.

This little town was no longer my home, but I had grown up here and periodically felt compelled to visit. I had driven a long way the day before and I wanted to spend some time at rest. But not more than twelve hours ago, upon my mother's incessant urging, I had decided to run this 5K race that began in the early hours of a Saturday morning. After my brother agreed, I too said yes, certain that I could run slow and steady.

My brother stood beside me, complaining in his jovial way how hot it was and how long it had been since he had run a race. We always did this, complained, to make the nervous energy disappear. Rather than talk about the impending race, we talked about the weather. My brother was tall, and he looked like a giant as he stood on the tips of his toes and stretched his arms high above his head.

The perspiration dampened his hair. He put his hands on his hips and twisted violently back and forth; I could tell he was anxious to get started.

"Do you know," my mother interrupted my thoughts as she sauntered to us, "that your little sister here ran *eighteen* miles yesterday? Before work?" She beamed at me and put her hand on my elbow to hold as if in a miniature hug. The motion pushed me and my foot instinctively took a quick step forward.

"Is that right?" My brother smiled at me, not at all intimidated. He wasn't listening. He never really did. But in his matter-of-fact way, he responded, without even looking at me. "Well, you're going to beat all of us then!"

"I doubt it," I said softly, embarrassed. "It was a tough run yesterday. Hot."

He turned from me. "Mom, then it's up to you to carry the family through this race." He smiled without looking at her either, and turned his attention to the man behind the bullhorn.

The gun fired. My legs, stiff and sore, slowly grew into the pace of the moving crowd. My brother ran beside me as we waved to my mother. She shooed us along, impatiently. She was too old for running this race but stepped into a brisk walk that was challenging even for her. As I instinctively glanced behind me, I watched my mother pump her arms and begin the 3.1-mile walk.

All my life my mother had been behind me. She had always been there, not always visible, but always in support, pushing me, encouraging me. Today was no different. She was the one who encouraged me to run this race, even though I pleaded with her to let me rest. When I told her I was too tired, she said "No way, a young girl like you? You can run this race. It's only a few miles. It'll be fun!"

I had relented. Maybe I just didn't want to let her down. Maybe I secretly wanted to be part of the activity. I don't know. I often did what I thought I should to please my family. It was a strange sensation since here I was, not even waiting for my mother when it was she who had brought me here. The sensation grew, and I knew that something was bothering me.

I always knew that my mother loved my brothers more. It was one of those things that all of us knew but never talked about except in jest. And now he was running beside me, one of my mother's two precious sons. I was just one of six girls, the last in a long line of frilly pink dresses, Barbie dolls, and unaccomplished goals. I had always been vocal about her overwhelming love for her sons. First I teased her about it, then I grew serious, then nonchalant. I realized that it had always been me who complained, anxious, jealous at the sight of my brother. Through the years, as my mother had so gallantly stood behind me, I felt that she was silently willing my brother to win. Maybe today I was determined to show her I could win.

I glanced at my brother, who was breathing hard now. I felt weightless as my legs fought with the burning muscles seeking revenge for the previous day's run. I also felt a little confused, wondering what made my brother so special and me so average. Although my muscles ached, in some strange independent way, I felt strong.

I concentrated on my pace. Even though I am usually too slow to win any race, my brother's pace had slowed tremendously and I was fighting the urge to go faster. He noticed this energy, either through his own exhaustion or my quick step, and urged me to go on. "Okay," I mumbled, breathing heavily, "but keep your pace—I won't be far ahead."

The air was thick and humid and it was difficult to go much faster. My shorts and top were soaked even before I passed through the sprinkler that some kind gentlewoman held out for our sweaty bodies. I have always wanted to be a boy, I thought, as I passed her. Then I laughed to myself. What a funny thought! I didn't want to be a boy in some strange sexual way; I just wanted to run faster, do more, have more opportunities. I think at that moment I just wanted to be my mother's son. And here he was, not more than a few minutes behind me, running as peacefully as could be.

I ran through the sprinkler, then turned and ran backwards a few steps to find my brother. I felt a compelling need to find him because in a moment of enlightenment, I realized that my brother had always understood what it meant to make the best of any opportunity. There was never any great need to compete. My mother had always stressed this point, and I finally understood, too.

I ran. If I was crying, the salty tears mixed with the perspiration and went unseen. I choked quietly but then resumed my steady breathing. My hand went to my face to wipe the sweat from my brow. I breathed deeply.

I could no longer see my mother, but I hadn't looked for her in the past mile. I realized that in my life there were plenty of times I couldn't see her, but I knew she was still there. She was probably finishing up her first mile as I started my last. My brother, somewhere in between, was still running strong. He was a strong soul. A strong peaceful soul.

My brother had never tried to beat me, but I, in retrospect, had always fought to be better than he was. The exception was basketball. We played our own version of the game in the pitch-black darkness of a cold winter's night. We couldn't dribble on the hard snow in northern Wisconsin, so we passed, shot, ran with the ball. He cried foul when he missed a shot and I'd let him shoot again. Silly me, letting him take all the good shots. I was just as capable.

I remember how my mother used to watch us from the small kitchen window, steam rising from the water in the sink and creating a great fog on the glass. We'd play for hours, and yet my mother always watched us. I, puny and uncoordinated, would struggle for the ball. My brother would tower over me and nearly knock me down as he lunged for a lay-up. I didn't want to embarrass Mom with my struggles, and I don't think I ever did, even when I knew I fell short of her expectations.

The pain in my legs turned into a dull ache as I approached the finish line. I was the first in my family to cross it and my hand went to my watch, automatically, as I pressed STOP. Twenty-seven minutes. Not a great time, but satisfactory for a recovery run. In a few more moments, I saw my brother running steadily. He looked great and I now knew why. He was at peace. He was happy. I cheered for him and said nice job when he, too, stopped and put his hands on his knees. When he stood I gave him a high five and we smiled a broad clean smile. We waited and paced, sweat streaming from our bodies as we caught our breath. Twenty minutes later, when my mother appeared, soaked from the perspiration that still lingered heavily on her skin, we congratulated her.

We exchanged information—the race, the results, the feeling of accomplishment. My brother was happy with his time and for some reason I knew he would be. He and I didn't win any awards, but in her age group, my mother won the gold medal. While the race directors passed out the accolades, my brother and I sat on the curb for a long while talking about the day. We talked about what brought us home and why. We even talked about Mom dragging us out of bed on a hot sunny morning to make us run a race. We laughed. My mother watched us silently as she walked around the area, so proud of her medal. She ended up wearing that medal all day and long into the night—the perfect reminder of a perfect day.

I had been first of the three of us to finish this race, just like I had been the first to do so many other things in our lives: attend graduate school, run a marathon, travel to the Far East. But it wasn't important anymore who was first or who was last. My mother was proud of us—both of us—and it had taken a silly little 5K race for me to realize this fact. For a few months I knew she would tell the story over and over again to anyone who would listen. I can hear her proud voice coming through strong: "I ran a race with my oldest and my youngest. I won a gold medal."

Years later, more peaceful and less wary, I would hear the story and I would be reserved, slightly embarrassed as she told the story to her same old-lady friends. Ultimately, when she had exhausted all versions of the story, complete with embellishments that so often accompany a story that is told over and over again, I was no longer a part. The story of my race would fall from her memory. She would remember my brother, but not me. And as I packed my bags to depart one last time, I felt melancholy, for still, at every point along the way, my mother had been behind me.

Dorothy Kangas grew up in a small northern Wisconsin town. The youngest of eight children, she claims she learned all-important life lessons from her family. She attributes her success at running, writing, and work to her family, including husband Bradley, son Jeremy, and dogs Scottie and Foster.

Donna-Lane Nelson

Real Life

Duckie!

Judith Ducker can't avoid her former classmate, who runs between two Chevy pickups to catch her. Trapped, Judith listens to the woman brag about her career, children, house, and husband.

"I'm just here seeing my folks. Then we're off to Europe. Ever been, Duckie?" the classmate asks. This summer Judith will be lucky to get to the beach two miles away.

The classmate kisses the air near Judith's cheek, an un-Maine action. As her classmate drives away in her Mercedes, Judith slips into the diner. "Sorry I'm late Tom."

"No problem," Tom says through the window between the counter and the kitchen. He is tapping out names onto a plastic strip. When he finishes, he hands her a badge.

Judith reads the blood-colored plastic: HI. MY NAME IS JUDY. She starts to say something, but Tom wipes his clean hands on his apron. Instead she pins the name tag to her uniform. As she puts clean ashtrays on the tables, she tries not to compare her life to her classmate's. What life, she thinks.

Only after her mother is in bed can she find time for herself.

Then she watches *MASH* and *Barney Miller* reruns, mouthing words with the performers. She knows all the *Star Treks* of any generation. When she watches TV, she imagines herself anyplace but Maine. She wonders how people find real lives. Hers is limited to working and caring for a woman sinking more into an unknown world each day.

As she tears open the first premeasured coffee packet of the fifty or more she will make during her shift she says, "Tom, I hate my job."

Tom says, "When ya quit give me plenty of notice."

"I don't want to quit." To quit she needs another job. To work in the insurance agency she'd have to type or use a computer. She can't do either. To clerk in Woolworth's, Smith's Pharmacy, or Jack's Grocery isn't that different from being a waitress at the Freetown Diner. The only other job is fishing. She gets seasick even watching swells from the dock. Seasickness isn't a family trait. Her father had been a fisherman for forty years before he drowned.

Freetown is a real Maine fishing village where the smells of dead fish and live lobsters drown out any odors of coffee. There isn't a boutique or an espresso bar within twenty miles. If tourists stop, they stay only long enough to decide there's nothing worth looking at.

When Judith feels more up she admits there are many things about her job she likes. Besides chatting up the fishermen she likes her nonfisherman customers like Fred. Once a week, after he picks up live lobsters to drive to Boston, he stops in. They talk about her mother and his wife who is undergoing chemo.

Judith likes watching kids convince their mothers to order Coke instead of milk. She likes knowing the main dish is pork pie on Monday, meat loaf on Tuesday, and lamb stew on Wednesday.

Looking out the window, Judith sees the first red leaves, although the green still heavily outnumber the red. It's August 25.

Midway through lunch Judith stares at the white milk on the counter, the sixth spill of the day. Automatically, she reaches for her rag.

"It's okay, Pete," she says to the five-year-old who upset his glass. Ketchup marks the corner of his mouth. He looks at his mother who'd slapped his hand. She's dabbing at the spill with the only two napkins available. Tom has told Judith to give one napkin with each meal. He thinks customers take too many when the dispenser is on the counter.

Judith throws the wet napkins in the trash then dips her milk-soaked rag in the water in the sink. There are only a few suds left; the rest have been driven out by a thin layer of grease.

"Time to pull the plug," she says to no one.

Judith gets home later than usual because Tom wanted the fryer washed. It had taken a long time to reassemble it. She also scrubbed the floor between the stools and counters with a brush instead of just mopping it.

Sandra, her sister-in-law, waits at the door, her jacket on. Judith senses her mentally tapping her foot. Sandra updates Judith over her shoulder as she rushes to her van. "Mother Ducker ate scrambled eggs for lunch. You need to give her a bath."

By 8 P.M. Judith is exhausted. Her mother, more agitated than usual, has wandered aimlessly from room to room, picking up knickknacks then putting them down again. She breaks the Hummel of a girl with an umbrella, the one Judith's uncle in the army sent from Germany. Although her mother got the dustpan, she forgot what she'd been doing. Judith cleaned up the smithereens.

After her mother falls asleep, Judith shoves a flat Orville Reddenbacher popcorn bag into the microwave her brothers gave her, she thinks to reduce their guilt for not helping more. She lets it nuke thirty seconds more than the instructions say because she likes it burned. She doesn't put it in a dish—one less thing to wash.

In the living room, Judith turns on a movie. She sits with her legs over one arm of the chair just as she did in childhood. The flowered slipcover is faded. Her mother made it ten years ago, the third for that chair.

The movie is a made-for-television rerun from the 70s. Joanne Woodward runs in the Boston Marathon. She finishes long after nightfall, one of the last to stumble across the line.

Judith crumbles the empty popcorn bag into a ball. She wonders how it feels to run. What made Joanne want to do it so badly? She thinks about it all the next day, even when seven-year-old David Andrews throws a hot dog at his six-year-old brother Josh and hits Judith instead. She washes the mustard and ketchup off her uniform. The spot stays darker pink than the rest of her uniform.

After her mother falls asleep, Judith channel-surfs. She can't forget Joanne Woodward's face as she fell across the finish line. Snap.

Judith shuts off the television.

Rummaging through her closet she finds a pair of five-dollar Woolworth's sneakers. She puts them on and adds a heavy sweatshirt.

She runs around the block several times, peeking in her mother's window every couple of rounds. From the night-light she can see her mother asleep. When Judith quits she breathes heavily, but she feels wonderful.

She is surprised her muscles don't hurt when she wakes the next morning. I must be in better shape than I thought, she thinks. She increases her laps by ten that night.

The next day her legs feel like someone snuck under the covers at night to twist each muscle. She hobbles around filling orders. Fred is there.

"Whatsa matter?" he asks.

"I don't want to talk about it," feeling too stupid to tell him. Instead of going home right after work, she goes to the library in Manascotport, the next town. She prays her Chevy won't break down on Route 1. This is the first time she has entered the library since her senior year in high school. The room hasn't changed. The librarian is the same except her hair is all gray.

"May I help you?" the librarian asks. Judith shakes her head no, because she is embarrassed to admit she wants to run a marathon.

An old wooden card catalog is across from the checkout desk. The smells of furniture polish and old paper remind her of her childhood. She finds five books about running. Three are out. She takes the two left.

Sandra says as Judith walks in late, "I'm going shopping." Her voice is icy like the time Judith forgot her birthday. She doesn't ask Judith if she needs anything. Judith sticks her tongue out as the van drives away.

She starts the wash. Her mother soils her bed nightly. The washing machine chugs. "Don't you dare give up," Judith says to it.

After her mother's bath, the two women pick over beans to bake. Judith's mother throws away the good ones and keeps the bad.

The second her mother is asleep Judith dives into her library books. She learns about warming up and pacing. She had tried to read earlier but her mother had wanted to look for Elsie, their St. Bernard who'd died ten years ago.

Over the weekend Judith drives her mother around the neighborhood to measure distances. Seven times around the block equals one mile. Running that night she wishes she could run in a straight line, but she must check her mother's window regularly. On her fifth lap she decides to run to and from work. Sandra always arrives after Judith leaves because Mrs. Ducker never wakes early. Leaving her mother alone for another half hour shouldn't cause a problem, she hopes. However, when the alarm goes off Monday at 4:30 instead of 5 A.M., Judith doubts the merit. Once moving along the road, she decides it was a good idea.

Fred passes her than stops his truck. "Wanta ride?"

"Nope, thanks. See ya later." She shifts her weight from foot to foot as they talk just as the library book suggested.

She is sweating when she arrives at the diner. Hurrying into the ladies room, she washes as best she can before changing into her uniform crammed into her backpack, which is the same color as her uniform. She doesn't remember buying it. Maybe it belongs to one of her sisters. One is on scholarship at the University of Vermont and the other is married to an air force captain and lives in Portsmouth, New Hampshire.

Fred sits at the counter, waiting for the lobster boats. "What were you doing running down the road?"

Judith debates telling him, but she's afraid of being mocked. Then she remembers the first day he'd come in he'd asked her name. He'd asked her if she preferred Judy or Judith. He's never called her Judy, even though most of the customers do. "I want to run in the Boston Marathon." She speaks softly so no one else will hear.

"That's great." Fred's smile says he means it. "You should ask them what you have to do to qualify."

"Yup." She wonders what she has to do.

Judith makes two phone calls to Boston. The first one is interrupted by her mother taking things out of the closet.

"I'll call you back," she says. Her mother can't remember what she was looking for. Together they put everything back. Judith puts her mother in front of a *Spenser for Hire* rerun and redials marathon headquarters.

"You should run some races first. Then a marathon. How old are you?" the professional voice asks.

"Forty."

"Qualifying time is 3:40." The voice tells Judith the nearest race is in Portland next month. Another race in Portsmouth in March. She has read about a local marathon two towns away in the local paper next to the article about a pet seal living down the coast.

When Judith asks her older brother to watch their mother during the races he says, "I've got a lot to do. Better not count on me."

Then she telephones her younger brother. When he says he can't, she gets angry. "Judy, you don't understand. I don't have the time. I've got a family."

"I'm beginning to think I don't," she says.

"Sis, someday, you'll get married," he says hanging up.

She looks at the phone. She doesn't run that night and drives to work the next day. Starting the first pot of coffee, she turns on the grill.

Fred comes in and throws his leg over the counter stool. "How's the running . . . coffee . . . hash browns . . . eggs . . . damn the cholesterol."

Judith shrugs. She puts Fred's order slip through the window for Tom. "I quit."

"You can't," he says.

"Yes I can." She tells him why.

"Don't let 'em use you . . . fight back," Fred says. "Don't take no for an answer . . . say no yourself," he says. Judith had never thought of saying no.

Judith calls her sisters during the low-rate time period. They're sympathetic, but the one in Portsmouth is nine months pregnant and the other has no money for bus fare from Vermont. They both offer to yell at their brothers.

Judith phones both brothers from the diner and tells them to come over that night. "Bring your wives," she says. Her hand shakes when she hangs up.

Sitting on the couch drinking tea from four unmatched mugs, Judith says to her brothers and Sandra, "I am going to run four marathons. If one of you don't stay with Mother, I'll walk out for good. Then she'll be your problem every day." Sandra especially looks upset. She is the next candidate to take full responsibility. She sloshes tea onto her jeans.

"You wouldn't do that," Judith's older brother says. He wears the red flannel shirt Judith gave him last Christmas. He always wears flannel shirts even when he takes Sandra out to the Dance and Dine on Route 1.

Her younger brother wears his police uniform. He is on duty. The cruiser is in front of the house. His wife is home with their three children.

Judith opens the closet. She pulls out the suitcase she packed early.

"Good-bye." She puts on her ski jacket.

"You wouldn't," her younger brother says.

"Here's a list of all the stuff you need to know about Mother. She puts five pages written both sides in her tight handwriting on the coffee table. "I'm outta here." Her car is half down the driveway before her younger brother runs after her. She stops and rolls down the window.

"You win," he says.

Judith sees his breath in the fall air. When he stands up his gun belt fills the window. She backs up into the garage. She is glad he stopped her since she had no place to go.

Judith finishes tenth from last in Portland's race. She finishes in the middle of the local marathon.

"You're wasting your time and ours," her older brother says. "You aren't winning. You're not even in the top ten."

"I'm finishing. Thank you for your support," she says.

Winter presents training problems. The first nor'easter dumps freezing rain the second week in November. A mile inland a foot of snow falls.

Although Judith tries to run, she twists her ankle and loses a week from both work and training.

Her brothers and sisters-in-law take care of both her and their mother. Judith ignores their complaints. None of them say "running" without "your stupid" in front of it.

Sitting with her bandaged ankle propped on a pillow Judith knows she can't stop training until spring. She sees an ad for a NordicTrack. Hobbling to the desk, she tries to figure out how to pay for it. There is no way, but the ad triggers an idea. When her ankle heals, she runs in place.

Judith's mother breaks her hip February 1 and is totally bedridden. Now Judith doesn't have to watch her as closely, but it means more work: keeping the bed fresh, massaging her limbs and rubbing her with oil to prevent bedsores.

As Judith runs in place each night she tries to remember how her mother used to be. The helpless woman is replaced by a younger woman making cookies and helping them put their tents up in the backyard. She hears her mother howl when she learned her husband would never come back from sea.

Judith once said to Sandra, "I didn't know we were poor until I was in high school." Sandra said it was a tribute to Mother Ducker.

Thus Judith prays with various degrees of guilt that the shell of her mother will die soon as she runs and thinks and thinks and runs.

Judith stays with her sister in Portsmouth for the March marathon. Her new niece has huge blue eyes.

Her sister and her brother-in-law watch the marathon and cheer Judith on. The day is cold and everyone is bundled in big cable sweaters, including the baby. They wear hand-knit peaked hats with pompoms. The baby nestles in a sling taking warmth from her father's body.

Judith wears old tights, shorts, a sweatshirt, and a head band. Soon the headband is too hot so she pulls it down around her neck. Some of the runners have expensive running outfits. Judith doesn't care about her clothes. All she wants is to finish so she can run in

Boston next month. Finishing a little ahead of middle place, she's happy her sister and brother-in-law think her running is "neat," not "stupid."

At the diner the Monday after the Portsmouth Marathon another man picks up the lobsters. The man has filled in for Fred before during vacations and emergencies. Judith had been looking forward to telling Fred she has qualified.

Tom hands Judith an order of waffles with sausages and another with two fried eggs, toast, and home fries. The plates are oval, not round, to hold more for big fisherman appetites.

The Fred substitute takes the waffles from Judith. He shakes his fingers after he puts the hot plate down. Then he drowns the waffles in Log Cabin syrup. He washes a mouthful of waffles down with the coffee.

"Where's Fred?" Tom asks.

"His wife died. He's taken the kids to Disney World."

"Strange," One fisherman says.

The substitute driver puts a whole sausage in his mouth. "His wife made him promise to do that. She was like that."

There is a moment of impromptu silence. Out of respect. Out of sympathy. Out of gratitude it's not them.

When Fred comes back in two weeks, Judith stammers out, "Sorry about the um, the um . . ."

"Thank you," Fred says. "Grilled cheese sandwich . . . sweet pickles on the side. . . . How ya getting to the marathon?"

"Bus, I guess. My junk heap won't make it."

"If you can get someone to stay with your mother for the week-end, you could ride down with me Friday . . . stay with me and the kids . . . save on a hotel. I live in Hopkinton."

"Hopkington?"

"Starting line."

"Fantastic." Judith stops. "Isn't it too soon after . . . um, I don't want to be in the way."

"Don't worry . . . do the kids good."

Judith's younger brother is angry to discover he'll be needed at the house Friday through Tuesday. Judith doesn't care. When he arrives, she shows him in minute detail how to change their mother.

"I can't do that!" he says. Judith pulls down the flannel night-dress hiding her mother's legs. She twists the baby-powder cap and sets it on the bureau.

"Why not? She changed you enough." She grabs her backpack and leaves.

Fred lives in a housing development built after the Korean War. When new, all the ranch houses looked alike, but as people added rooms, garages, and landscaping the homes took on different per-sonalities. Fred's is green.

His two kids, Allison and Nathan, greet them at the door. "It's fantismo you're running the marathon," Allison says using the slang she'd learned in seventh grade that day. Nathan, four years younger, says nothing. Judith will sleep in Allison's room. "You want the top or bottom bunk?" Allison asks as she throws three sweaters, dirty underwear, and jeans off a chair so Judith can sit. "I'm sorry my room is such a mess."

"My room was worse at your age, and it's not much better now."

"Really?"

"Really!" Judith says.

Nathan knocks at the door. "You guys want to eat at Burger King? Dad says we can if Judith says okay."

As Judith put the last french fry into her mouth, Fred gives her a map of the race route. "Tomorrow you can use my car to drive the route."

"Can I go with you?" Nathan asks.

"Of course," Judith says.

"Me, too. Daddy can finish digging," Allison says.

Fred had told Judith he'd put off most yard work for two years. "I doubt if I'll get it all done tomorrow, but at least I'll get the plants in before they die in the pots," he says. He turns to Judith. "Leave the kids if you want to go alone."

"Are you kidding? I need navigators. I don't do cities," she says.

Allison cooks dinner the night before the race. She forbids anyone entry into the kitchen. Fred explains how Allison took over the cooking when his wife was ill.

By the time the teenager calls them into the dining room, there's a white tablecloth on the table. A salad bowl sits next to a large casserole with tomato sauce. Two cardboard cylinders on each end of the table are marked KRAFT PARMESAN CHEESE. They're bright green like the house.

Allison carries a plate from the kitchen piled high with spaghetti. "You need lots of carbohydrates," she says.

Judith smiles. "I heard you're a good cook."

"Mom taught me." A heaviness coats the room.

"It's tough taking care of a sick mother even when you're my age," Judith says. Fred explains that Judith's mother is very sick.

Monday morning, Marathon Day, Judith wakes at 5 A.M. Getting out of bed she limbers up in the living room. Fred drives her to the starting line where she gets her number—654. Thousands of runners mill around. Wheelchairs are everywhere. The chair racers have a marathon starting immediately before the regular race.

A woman who looks at least fifty-five runs in place. She says without stopping that this is her sixth marathon. "I started running when I was fifty-four—ten years ago."

About five minutes later a man with gray hairs sticking over his shirt says to Judith, "You know the woman you were talking to? She's a nun."

Judith listens to bits of conversations.

"It's a good day. Not too hot," someone says.

"Remember the year it was ninety?"

"Yah, and the next year it snowed."

Everyone is in various stages of warming up. Finally they take their places.

The starting gun fires. Judith finds a comfortable pace. This is the densest race she has run in, a contrast to her lonely night running. As Judith runs past the crowd hollering encouragement she thinks in amazement *I'm really here*. I'm running the Boston Marathon. I'm like Joanne Woodward. Then she smiles. Only without Paul. She puts away images of the Newmans to concentrate on breathing.

In Natick she sees Nathan, Allison, and Fred. They wave. Nathan breaks into a run and gives her some water from a paper cup. "See you in Newton," he says.

In Newton the kids jump up and down as Judith runs by. "Atta girl, Judith," Fred calls.

Heartbreak Hill looms in front of her. She's next to the nun. A man ahead of her falls. He shakes his head and limps to the side. Judith runs on, ignoring the growing pain in her muscles.

Two men with video cameras train their lens on her. One is an amateur. The other camera has CHANNEL 5 on it. A commentator talks into a microphone. Judith wonders if she'll be on television as she crosses the crest of Heartbreak Hill. Fred is recording the television coverage on his VCR.

As she crosses the Boston city line she sees the Prudential Tower. The finish line is in front of the skyscraper. The crowds have become deeper. The nun is still beside her. "We'll make it," the nun gasps.

Every muscle in Judith's body aches. She wants to cry. The sky has gotten darker and suddenly it pours. Steam rises off the runners' bodies. Most of the crowd runs for cover.

She remembers a story her mother read her about a little train that went up a very high hill to bring milk to the good little boys and girls in the city. It kept saying "I think I can, I think I can." Judith doesn't have to think she can. She knows she can.

Fred and the kids hold wet copies of the *Boston Globe* over their heads. There are very few people left in the stands, the rest having scattered from the torrential rain.

Judith sees them as she crosses the line. Fred holds her jacket as they make their way to her.

"Fantismo," Allison says as Fred wraps her jacket around her shoulders. "You were 275th and the 35th woman," Allison says.

"Totally awesome," Nathan says.

Judith pants too hard to speak. She wonders what she needs to do to beat her record in the next marathon.

Donna-Lane Nelson is an American living in Switzerland. Her stories and poems have been published in six countries and read on BBC World Radio. She has an M.A. in creative writing from the University of Glamorgan in Wales.

Rebecca Davis

Running Romances

I've met the great loves of my life while running; I share a special bond with those who know that limbs whirling through space make everything about body and soul happy. But mine are no ordinary loves—I've never been asked to share a Gatorade with a man I've met running, much less dinner and a movie. Yet I've been romanced and all across the country by another running breed, that most natural of runners and affectionate of species, the dog. Fred and Tam, Harvest and Bristol, Red, Tang, Mocha, and now Hans and Cassie have run tight circles around my heart and our woman-dog affairs have ranged from tragic to comfortable to wildly ecstatic. The equation has been simple: Dogs love to run, I run, dogs love me. I've met my sweethearts in the Southwest, New England, the Midwest, and now California, and each one of them has notched my heart.

Like many people, I first fell in love during my freshman year at college. I was going to school in New Mexico, and would run across the arroyos and through the town of Santa Fe. I trained heavily in those days, running six to twenty miles every morning. One morning as I finished my run I noticed a fight breaking out at the campus soccer field. A knot of snarling dogs had encircled two others; all of them were large, seventy- to eighty-pound shepherd-husky mixes common to the New Mexico hills. The two victims were no smaller than their oppressors, and though they did not look browbeaten, they were outnumbered.

I may have been stupid, but dogs scared me less than people, so I jumped into the fray. I could not stand to see these animals get hurt. I waved my arms wildly, shouted and hooted, and somehow managed to break the spell of danger. The dog gang fled, and the two that had been threatened remained. These two dogs seemed to be all right; I saw no bites or wounds. I clucked over them and patted them; they were not wild or afraid. When I turned to walk back to my dormitory room they trotted along beside me for a while, then dropped back and disappeared.

The next morning as I ran past the soccer field, the two dogs I'd rescued emerged from under the bushes that lined the road. They must have been waiting. These two dogs ran happily with me for the entire six-mile route. From that time on, they rarely left my side. Both the dogs had collars, so I knew they had a home. A dull red heart hung from the smaller dog's neck, but it was not inscribed. I called them Fred and Tam, and they would wait outside the dorm for me, follow me to the cafeteria, escort me to my classrooms—I was soon known to the entire campus as "the girl with the dogs."

I had no idea when Fred and Tam ate but they looked healthy enough that I was certain they went home sometime to be fed. When I returned from holiday and summer breaks, "my" dogs would inevitably show up on my first day back. Tam was a young female, I guessed that she was maybe two or three. Fred was much older, perhaps closer to nine or ten, though he had as much running stamina as Tam. Both dogs would run with me for up to twenty miles in the hot New Mexico sun without faltering.

Fred and Tam were able to repay me for their soccer field rescue within a year of our first acquaintance. One morning a truck filled with inebriated, frightening cowboys began to drive along beside me as I ran. It was six o'clock in the morning and there were no other cars on the road—I was seven or eight miles outside of Santa Fe. The men in the truck began to hoot and jeer at me. I wasn't certain if they were trying to hit me with the truck or if they were simply taunting me, but the words became more and more threatening.

I was beyond nervous and decided that the best thing to do was get off the road to where the truck couldn't follow. I plunged down an arroyo. My dogs followed. Incredibly, so did the truck—though it didn't get far. I heard the truck door open, and one of the men began to run after me. I swore to myself as the man lurched forward. He was surprisingly fast. And that is when Tam and Fred returned the favor I'd done them when we first met. They somehow sensed that these men were trying to hurt me and they turned, snarling and growling. They chased the man back into the truck as I ran up and out of the arroyo. My dogs—for that is what I called them by that time—caught up with me later and when we finally got back to the dorm I collapsed with them on my mattress and cried and hugged them.

After Fred and Tam had been with me for almost two years, I

found out about their lives. I was walking in downtown Santa Fe and they, of course, were following me. I heard the cry of "Gordo! Gordo!" behind me. *Gordo* is Spanish for "fat" so I was hoping this person wasn't yelling at me. But the cry was insistent, and so I finally turned. A man came running up and went, not to me, but to Fred. He explained that Fred and Tam were his dogs—Fred's real name was Gordo, Tam's was Bloom.

This man said he'd wondered why in the last two years his dogs had been gone so much; he hadn't realized that they'd fallen in love. I was glad they had a home, glad to finally meet the other part of their lives. I had been worried about them because I was planning to transfer to a college in Vermont, and though I knew that somehow those two dogs would survive, I feared they only had me to love them. The man asked me if I fed them, hinting that he'd sure like to see them more. I told him that I didn't feed them though I don't know that he believed me. I suggested that he take up running—told him that the way to these dogs' hearts wasn't through the stomach, but through the road. I hope that when I left he began to run with them.

I was sad to say good-bye to a lot of friends when I left, but my saddest good-bye was that final run with Fred and Tam. I trusted that they would run many, many more miles, and I still hold them in my heart, knowing that ours was a romance that transcended puppy love.

In Vermont I was adopted by two smaller dogs—an Irish setter and a small mutt of indeterminate origin. I knew that both of these dogs had a home from the get-go. Harvest, the Irish setter, lived in a house where I shared space with a troupe of puppeteers. Bristol, Harvest's best friend, came from three doors down. The three of us had a wonderful time running the rolling hills of Vermont. In the winter we plowed through the snow tracks that cars had left. Fortunately, these were easy loves—we had no horrifying adventures, no dramatic rescues. Ours was a comfortable romance—less exciting than my infatuation with Fred and Tam, but pleasurable for its consistency and certainty.

Then came Red. Red is the love of my life, the dog I will never quite get over. We met in Massachusetts, where I worked during the summers as a puppeteer. I was running on the roads that circle the cranberry bogs outside Plymouth when I first encountered him. I was midway through my run when I spotted a deer in the field before me. I thought it odd that the deer hadn't bolted as I approached. Then I realized that this was no deer—it was a Doberman pinscher. The biggest Doberman I'd seen in all my life. I'd only seen Dobermans in the movies or tightly restrained by fierce-looking men dressed in leather and metal. I slowed my pace a little because I didn't want the dog to smell my fright. But I had to get past him, and running in the opposite direction seemed unwise. He began to lope toward me. I jogged oh so slowly; unable to stop my mind's moviehouse from running all the scenes of snarling Dobies I could conjure.

The giant red Doberman stopped and then turned as I passed. I winced as he wheeled around, expecting a chunk of my bottom to be chomped at any moment. Out of the corner of my eye I saw that he was not licking his chops, but running gracefully at my side.

And we ran in tandem for the next two or three miles. The same phenomenon occurred that had happened with Fred and Tam. Every day, this dog would find me and we would run together. I quickly met his owner, Bob, a man who repaired cars. Bob and I established a relationship in which I ran Red back to his house after we'd finished our morning constitutional. Red fell utterly in love with me, and I in turn lost my heart to him. I lived in a trailer park and in the morning Red would come to find me. He would sit exactly underneath whatever spot in the trailer I happened to be. If I shifted, he would shift. Even if there were other people in the trailer, Red knew which heartbeat was mine.

Sometimes I would pull out my bike and ride five miles to the Miles Standish State Forest, then another five miles on the bike trails and five miles back home. Red would run faster than I could pedal for the entire time. Once when it began to rain, Red and I huddled under a picnic table together till the storm let up, he panting in my lap and I hugging him. This dog was built to run and he gloried in it.

Red would follow me to the park where I performed the puppet shows, but I would have to tie him behind the puppet truck because children were scared of him. Then I'd run him home between breaks in the shows. Bob was a nice man, and he saw how Red and I loved each other. He told me that when I finished college and returned the following year, I could have Red. He thought that we should be together. Difficult as it would be to house and feed the world's biggest Doberman pinscher when I was a poor art student, I agreed that this should happen. Red and I were meant to be together. It was impractical but necessary.

The next year when I returned, I looked for Red. He didn't bound out from his yard that first morning that I called for him. So that afternoon I went to see Bob.

"Where's Red?" I asked.

"I had to put him to sleep," he said.

I was dumbfounded. Red had only been four or five years old. Bob explained that Red had killed some of the neighbors' chickens, Bob was being threatened if he didn't deal with the problem. He didn't have my phone number; he hadn't been able to call me. I was stunned. Couldn't he have kept Red inside, kept him in a fenced yard? Bob shook his head. You know how he was—like a deer. He loved to run.

It took me a long time to get over Red. I had Tang, and Mocha—my landlords' dogs in Boston and in Minneapolis—to run with me. But it was not the same. Red had chosen me. Then I moved to California, bought a house, and for the first time chose a dog of my own, a collie puppy I could train to run with me. Cassie, a beautiful Lassie look-alike, is now five years old, and I've trained her to run beside me since she was nine months old (the bigger the dog the longer you have to wait before you let them run seriously— has to do with bone development, I believe). Three years later we added Hans, also a collie—turns out I like the breed—but of a startling coloration. He's called a blue merle, and is black and gray and white with one blue eye and one brown eye. Cassie is now five and Hans is one and a half.

Where my other running pals ran free beside me, Cassie and

Hans have to run on a leash most of the time, as California roads are more hectic. Cassie is an almost ponderously slow jogger who makes frequent stops to inspect, sniff, and puzzle over plants and shrubs of all varieties. Hans is a hard-charging athlete who wants nothing more than to run at breakneck speed for miles at a time, pausing only when a sprinkler starts to spurt or a cat runs across the street—well, it's less a pause than a skid and jerk. For the first time ever I am getting an arm workout as well as a leg and heart workout as I run, my arms pulled apart in an incredible stretch as I urge Cassie forward while reeling Hans back. It's different, choosing a dog rather than having a dog choose you, but in urban territory dogs aren't roaming around looking for friends and runners.

Cassie and Hans stand on my chest each morning, licking me feverishly till I arise. They watch me alertly as I brew coffee and read the morning paper. They both know that the minute I crease the paper in half and walk to the garage to dump it in the recycle bin the time has come. They both dance and chortle expectantly, Cassie whining softly and Hans puffing his cheeks out and chattering his teeth in anticipation. They know that it is time for the morning run. We all three bolt out the front door in a blend of pure human-canine joy, the shadows of all my dogs accompanying us as we gallop down the street.

Rebecca Davis is a writer, painter, former puppeteer, and dog lover living in Fremont, California. She has written two books, Birdskins *and* Aya, *and has published several short stories. She has been running for almost twenty years.*

Susan Marsh

Into the Light

At the Hyalite Lake trailhead, I stopped the car under a tall spruce. A discarded walking stick was propped against the trail sign, the only evidence that others had been here. Glad to have the mountains to myself, I pulled on my rucksack. Its solidity offered a welcome illusion of support, as if someone were standing behind and holding me up. I tugged the waist strap tight and started up the trail.

I came for refuge from a vague emotional turmoil that had built all summer. Lately it loomed like a shadow half obscured by mist, with no single cause that I could recognize or name. I longed for friends, tired of bumping against the fringes of Bozeman's tight-knit social scene like a fly bouncing off a window. An already fierce relationship with my boss had erupted into a shouting match in the office. I had just paid my first visit to a counselor. I don't know why I'm here, I told her, but my life is just a mess.

After I rattled on for ten minutes, she peered at me and asked, Do your parents drink?

I left her office angry. Yes, they drink, I had said. But what did that have to do with me? No answers came, but something urged me to find a forest trail where I could run. By instinct I understood it would help. The cool indifference I could not bear in other people gave comfort when it came from the mountains.

I had been running daily since snow left the Gallatin Valley in April, running away from pain and confusion. After the first few minutes I would find my stride. My mind shifted into neutral, empty of disturbing thoughts. I ran for the chemicals of well-being released by my brain, the sense of clarity they gave. I found myself running farther and more often, desperate for that clarity.

Soft with rotted wood, familiar as an old sweater, the wide trail led into the dusk of early morning. The patch of light at the trailhead receded to a distant point behind me. A small creek tumbled beneath a thicket of alder in muffled counterpoint to the silent forest.

A loud burst of machine-gun chatter spun me around. A squirrel scolding. It peered at me with its tail curled into a question mark as if to ask, Jumpy today, are we? Then it scuttled up a tree.

Yes, jumpy. And irritable. What's your problem? I snapped.

Jogging along with my head bowed, I let a stream of self-accusations flow, determined not to let another squirrel interrupt. I passed a lovely waterfall and did not even glance in its direction. I had seen it many times. Besides, the tumult in my head boiled louder than the falls. I was well into my standard litany of what was wrong with me. Word for word, I replayed the fight with my boss, feeling my face flush at the memory. Liar, he had called me. Anger spurred me into a canter.

Hooking my thumbs into the shoulder straps of my rucksack to keep it from bouncing, I glanced at the firm muscles pumping below my hiking shorts. The ease with which my legs took me up a mountain trail usually brought satisfaction and confidence. But now I just compared them to my failures. If my ability to shut my mouth and get along with people were running, I would be a stumbling fool. My condemnations became more pointed, as if I were trying to hurt my own feelings with their sting. I ran faster.

The trail began to climb. The gentle track that could hold two abreast now cut a steep, narrow bevel in the mountainside. Boulders jutted from the trail and gullies carved its center. My agitated jog slowed as I was forced to watch my step. Breath came deeper as the pulse pounded in my neck and chest. Moisture collected under my rucksack.

I raced the sun as its rays spilled over the canyon rim and the thick-trunked spruces gave way to subalpine fir. Open slopes marked the paths of winter avalanches. Above their fringes of grass, clusters of Indian paintbrush flared like torches, leading me into the light.

With a shortened stride against the steep trail, I reined in my breathing to match my footsteps. Long ago I had learned to combat side stitches by breathing in for three steps then exhaling slowly over the next three. I listened for the rhythmic slap-slap-slap of my feet, then took the welcome measured breath.

Above the curving tree trunks, above the glowing wildflowers, the slope broke, leaving only sky. The sky, my destination. With each switchback the cliffs swelled more fully into view. The wide glacial trough of Hyalite Canyon snaked to the north, opening like unfolding hands onto the Gallatin Valley. Far below, the metal roof of a farm building glinted. Hay fields ran in long blond patches. The paths of creeks flowing from the mountains twisted into ribbons of green. Above the valley, the Bridger Range cut the northern horizon into a series of conical humps.

My pent-up rage gathered with each breath: step, step, step. Liar! I pushed it out and ran beyond its poison: step, step step. Bullshit!

The taut spring inside began to uncoil as I ran toward the sky. Anger dissipated like a mist. The office where I worked was lost in distance, the town nothing more than a patch of green on the far side of the hayfields. From here I looked down upon my boss as if from heaven. This change in perspective rendered him remote and unimportant.

The forest broke into scattered clusters of subalpine fir. I glanced backward only at the Bridgers, forward only as far as the next switchback. When I stopped for breath at an overlook I counted five waterfalls, one so close it filled the air with noise and mist, the others tumbling from distant rims, gushing white but silent. Slowly, my litanizing mind left behind the boss. It left behind the counselor with her penetrating eyes, waiting to tell me more of what I was afraid to hear. The Bozeman cliques spun their webs of petty intrigue without me. None of them mattered anymore.

The trail led to the knobby rim of a scoured glacial cirque. I turned north at its brink for another look at the Bridgers, receding now that I had reached the same elevation as their highest peaks.

Beside me, the subalpine firs pointed at the sky like minarets. Look up, their silhouettes suggested. Notice this brilliant August day, a day like no other. I noticed.

In the cirque basin, Indian paintbrush spread a palette—scarlet, magenta, tangerine orange, pale yellow. One kind grew short and dense, another tall and spiky. I cataloged their details and wondered if they were each a different species. The variations of paintbrush became the sole focus of my interest. I could not remember when I had stopped lecturing myself.

The sun was high, close to noon. I peeled from the trail and cut across the wildflowers to the shore of Hyalite Lake. I dropped my rucksack and splashed into the water. I poured cool handfuls over my head, then found a log seat and pulled the Rye Crisp and cheddar from my pack. The water I carried was still cold, unopened. I took a long drink and assembled lunch.

Hyalite Lake was a saucer of turquoise set into the gold of August meadows. A sandpiper skimmed its surface like a skipping stone. Above the lake, an amphitheater of rimrock cupped the sky. Stringers of alpine rush, bronzed by early frost, reached into the talus on the crest of the Gallatin Range, where even at midday the peaks cast long shadows. The sun's warmth soaked into my legs. A cool breeze crept along my spine. The inner coil continued to unwind, leaving me with only a vague weariness, no words left rattling in my head.

Food and rest refreshed me. The lake was lovely, an adequate destination, but I still hungered for higher ground. The main trail zigzagged up the shoulder of Hyalite Peak. I considered it, then remembered a little-used route leading to the Squaw Creek Divide.

The unmarked and discontinuous path skirted knobs of bedrock and dipped into lush swales. Where the meadow grew thick, the trail disappeared. No blazes scarred the trees, no rock cairns pointed the way. I scanned the mountain to the west for clues, then plunged across the meadow toward the base of a bouldery slope. The same attention that had shown me variations in Indian paintbrush served me now: at the far end of the meadow, I found the trail slanting faintly up a hem of scree.

Again I climbed, but slower now, exhilarated from my five-mile run. Slabs of cleaved-off bedrock formed the trail, ringing like china underfoot. The naked talus shuffled down the mountain, collecting no soil. Some of the boulders contained holes formed by gas bubbles trapped when the molten basalt cooled and thickened. The vesicles had since filled with a pearly white form of opal. Hyalite. It blinked from the dull gray slabs. Pearls of it littered the trail. I picked one up and held it into the light, where it flickered with a trace of pale carmine fire.

As I approached the mountain's spine, the slope became gentler, the scree no longer on the move. The angular slabs settled into nests of rush and mountain heather. Clumps of purple-flowered sky pilot sent their skunky aroma across the trail as I turned the final switchback onto a long ridge. The trail squeezed through a cliff band onto the Gallatin Divide.

Distant mountains bounced into view. Across the Gallatin Canyon, the Spanish Peaks bristled with spires. Squaw Creek ran to the west, its upper reaches hidden by the mountain under my feet as it steepened out of sight. A silvery crew cut of grass outlined the break in slope. On the east side of the ridge, Hyalite Lake lounged with its feet up, a pool of Caribbean green. Shadows crept like timid swimmers from the shaggy pines along its shore.

The trail dropped into Squaw Creek. I left it to stay on the ridge, strolling along with a light and casual step. I had reached my destination. I closed my eyes to feel the warm sunlight on their lids.

A squarish block of basalt presented itself, the perfect seat. I dropped my pack and drank again, then sat with my hands on my knees, staring. How long had it been since I ran up a mountain, where no one knew where I was? I could lie back and stare at nothing for the next hour, or walk for miles down the mountain crest. Either way, I could disappear. With no one probing or peering over my shoulder—Liar! Do your parents drink?—I began to enjoy my own company. I wanted nothing, my mind uncluttered and clear.

My once-troublesome side stitches had vanished after I learned how to breathe in rhythm with my stride. Now I saw I could use the same idea to combat brain stitches. Get the mind in rhythm with the body. As my legs focused on their task of getting me up the mountain, all parts had to cooperate. This was no place for the brain to be off on some melancholy tangent; its job was to watch for rocks in the trail and the varying details of Indian paintbrush.

I wasn't running away from problems anymore, but toward a solution. I couldn't see it yet, but I knew it lay in front of me, and I felt myself closing in. Moments of clarity, when lungs and heart and legs and mind worked together, were accumulating in my memory. They were helping me become whole, a puzzle piece at a time. On the ridge above Hyalite Lake, I began to see that by running, I was healing myself. I felt like an insect emerging from its brittle carapace.

The image of shedding skin gave me an idea. I untied my boots and pulled them off. Cool air bathed my damp feet. I peeled off my socks and laid them on a rock, wriggling my toes into the soft mats of heather. It felt delicious—I wanted more. I pulled the sweaty T-shirt over my head and slipped out of my shorts and underwear.

My clothing and boots on a rock, I walked away. I started to tell myself this was crazy. What was I doing wandering around with nothing on, at ten thousand feet in the Montana sky? But it didn't feel crazy. It was the sanest thing I had done all summer. At last my mind was still, and my senses feasted. I raised my arms to feel the sun on skin stretched tight across my collarbone. The breeze lifted the fine hairs along my flanks. I noticed my tanned and muscular legs, ready to take me anywhere. Pain and anger floated into the August sky above that black-rocked precipice until they disappeared.

The sun dipped low to the west as I picked my way down the music-making scree. I started into the switchbacks and the dark gorge of Hyalite Canyon. A breeze stirred at the back of my neck. Joyfully, I broke into a run.

Susan Marsh has been writing articles and essays since the mid-1970s. Recently, she has focused on personal essays and memoir. Her work has appeared in Orion, North Dakota Quarterly, Wyoming, Northern Lights, *and other magazines and anthologies. She has lived in Jackson, Wyoming, since 1988.*

MaryAnne Chute Lynch

Stepping onto the Moon Barefoot

I took it for granted that I could enter the 101st Boston Marathon without disguising myself as a man, the way Katherine Switzer, the first female competitor did. I was not worried about being yanked off the 26.2-mile course because a race official detected I was female.

My first attempt at Boston was a celebration, marking the twenty-fifth year of women running the race. My children asked me why women weren't allowed in the Boston Marathon until twenty-five years ago. It is peculiar to them because it is their two aunts, not their six uncles, whom they've watched in marathons and triathlons. They saw their female kindergarten teacher run her eleventh marathon in Boston, and they tracked me as I took on a race I feared was out of my league. When I registered for my Boston race, I was unaware it was a momentous occasion, or that my running might be perceived as feminism.

Feminism has become somewhat of a curse word in the last decade, while *feminine* has seen a marketing resurgence. Advertisers deftly capitalize on the financial gains women made through feminism's initial thrust. But they persist in barraging us with products that extol an icon of feminine that never has and never will exist. This virtual-reality female exercises a fat-free body without sweating or developing foot odor, has a dynamic career, drives a spotless vehicle wearing silk garments that kids never bleed or rub their noses onto, and has family members who all eat the same food at supper.

Not my everyday scene, nor an image manifest at the marathon. Nevertheless, running in Boston made me realize how riddled I am by both feminine and feminist forces. I never thought I would come near the qualifying time for the Boston Marathon, so I never tried. When I was told that I made the cut off in a qualifying race, I said, I couldn't have. My qualifying marathon must have been two or three miles short of twenty-six.

The idea still can't register in my head; it pops out like bread in a toaster that won't stay down. My mind imagines that the Boston Athletic Association may soon tighten the qualifying times if amateurs of my ilk can get into the competition.

Despite months of twelve-to-twenty-mile conditioning runs prior to the race, I worried whether or not I would make it up Heartbreak Hill. I couldn't squelch my doubts. Is this quintessential female thought or is it my own invention?

Boston was the third marathon I completed. Yet when colleagues ask me about my running, I laugh and tell them, I trot. I consider myself a jogger and I train at dawn so as not to be on public display. I am not a zealot who reads running books and magazines, trains on hills, does sprints, uses sports gels, and lives the sport. Is that the feminine aspect, the brainwashed girl in me who still thinks it is shameful to beat Mark or Ross in the relay races at school if you want them to let you play Wiffle ball on the street?

And what about my not wanting to look like the only dumpling lacing my sneakers among the taut string beans at the start? Yes, these images still haunt me, ever taunt me. It may take me a lifetime to resolve these nemeses.

Until I was ten, I thought every adult female had a belly like a beach ball, pushed a baby carriage, ironed men's shirts, and cooked roasts like my mother and the women in my neighborhood. When I first saw a marathon, I wondered if women were allowed in the race or if a woman could endure it. Lining up at the start in Boston was, for me, equal to joining an Apollo crew and stepping onto the moon barefoot.

My twin daughters, however, saw my first marathon when they were three, after which they began running up and down empty grocery store aisles until breathless, saying to each other, "Great race! That was my first marathon! All my toenails turned black!"

How different their view of their place in the world will be or already is, as indicated in their reaction to this anniversary event. I am encouraged that after watching hundreds of women, salty, chafed and euphoric with challenge, my children think it bizarre that females were barred from the Boston race. I hope subliminal advertising, unequal pay, anorexic models, and banter over feminism will seem equally absurd to their children in twenty-five years.

MaryAnne Chute Lynch is a freelance writer who focuses on health, science, and consumer issues. She began marathon running after her three daughters and one son were born.

Bharti Kirchner

Running Bangladesh

In my youth I had lived for several years in Bangladesh. The society, then, was steeped in tradition. Women concealed themselves in *borkhas,* body veils, and few went for athletics. So recently, when planning a stopover in Dhaka, Bangladesh's capital, on the way to my native India, I wondered if I could explore it by running as I usually do in my travels. Bangladeshi expatriates in the United States assured me the running craze had reached there. In my mind I questioned whether women took part. Finally I decided I wasn't going to let old ways stop me.

As I left the Dhaka airport, I watched carefully for signs of current mores regarding women and sports. The day was hot and everyone seemed to be out, crowding the wide boulevards. Fewer women now wore *borkhas;* most were clad in saris that covered their bodies from head to toe. And sure enough there were no women runners on the road. So I figured a track away from the public eye would be the best. How would I locate one? I called a Bangladeshi friend from the hotel.

"I'll be right over," he said enthusiastically. "To show you around. And we'll find a place you can run."

We rode a bicycle rickshaw to the old part of the city—a trading post of the sixteenth-century Mughal kings. The narrow, crowded lanes were filled with small businesses. I saw a tailor sewing cotton pants, an artisan carving designs on conch shell, a vegetable vendor weighing jewel-like dots of shelled peas. We stopped at the stall of a fruit juice vendor. On learning I was a tourist, he gave me a second helping of coconut water and began telling me of the origin of the city's name.

Centuries ago, his story went, a conqueror's emissary landed here and at first could see only jungles. Then he discovered a scenic hamlet. "Oh! the hidden beauty!" he exclaimed. He named the place Dhaka, a word meaning "covered."

I was charmed by the story, but knew Old Dhaka wasn't the place for me to run. Shortly after, my friend escorted me to the new section of the town. He proudly pointed to their version of a shopping mall, an aged building with chipped paint on its wall. For a country that has existed for several thousand years, *new* is a relative term. On one of the upper floors was located a restaurant named Prince that was packed with people and smelled of thousand spices. From the dome of a mosque in view, I could hear the call to prayer. A rickshaw stand sported dozens of waiting rickshaws, and a open market buzzed with activities, selling everything from clothes to frying pans. I was seeing everyday life in Dhaka. Was there a running spot somewhere?

"And there is the stadium," my friend said, pointing to a high brick fence. "Is there an athletic field here?" I asked, thinking he must not have understood what I wanted.

Smiling, my friend steered me through an opening. Inside was a large soccer field with a few benches for spectating.

"You can run here tomorrow morning," he said. "The gate is opened early."

I could hardly wait. What a perfect place for running, away from the public eye.

The next morning I rose early. Near the hotel entrance I spotted a single rickshaw puller and signaled him. Right away he objected to taking me to the stadium. "No, no," he kept saying, shaking his head without explaining.

My enthusiasm floundered, but I kept insisting. Reluctantly, after arguing, he agreed. Did he know something I didn't? Nervously, I climbed the passenger's seat.

The man dropped me off near the stadium. Few people were out on this cloudy morning at this early hour. I entered the field, empty except for a few crows, flying overhead. Taking off my jacket, I placed it on grass and looked around once more. Still no one in sight. I started to run in the central part, going around and around. After a few minutes, sunlight peeked through the clouds, dissipating my unease. Just the sun, the sky, and me: I could have been anywhere in the world. I picked up my speed and felt energized for a three-mile run, which would take many laps.

Halfway through, I noticed a few men gathering near the gate. Who are these men? I wondered. Curious observers? Religious zealots?

Soon there were about fifteen of them, strong, vigorous looking, watching me. A few seated themselves on the bench, like this was a show to watch. Best to keep running, I decided. As far as I could see, there seemed no way out of the place except having to go past them.

But my mind wouldn't rest. Would they throw stones at me, a woman breaking tradition? Detain me in jail for running? I rounded the curve, picturing a headline from Dhaka's daily newspaper: WOMAN ARRESTED FOR VIOLATION OF SOCIAL CODES.

"She was wearing a short sleeved shirt, baggy pants, running in a circle, and sweating." I saw the lead line in the article. On shaky legs, I continued.

Suddenly, a single male voice broke through my thoughts. "Bravo, bravo," he yelled, followed by applause, then cheers that grew louder and louder. I could hardly believe a middle-of-the pack woman runner like me with only age-group medals to my credit, was being honored by men with cheers and applause, the kind normally reserved for a world-class racer. I'd never think of myself as an ordinary runner.

Feeling like an Olympian, I completed my last lap. I threw my jacket over my shoulders and walked toward the gate to leave.

The men surrounded me. "What is your name? Where are you from? Do you run competitively?" they wanted to know.

Their grins got even bigger when I answered them in Bengali. They were soccer players, I learned, who practiced there every morning. Out of respect for me they had waited until I finished.

"Visit us again soon!" they said, spreading out for their practice runs.

The same rickshaw puller was waiting. He smiled and took me

back to my hotel. It occurred to me that earlier he had been uncomfortable about taking a woman alone.

I felt like that conqueror of long ago who had named the city Dhaka. All because of a run. And for the rest of my stay, I savored the city's hidden beauty through many more laps.

Bharti Kirchner is the author of six books. Two of the books are novels: Shiva Dancing *(1998) and* Sharmila's Book *(1999), both published by Dutton. She has published four cookbooks, including* The Bold Vegetarian *(HarperPerennial, 1995). She has also published dozens of articles and essays in publications such as* Writer's Digest, Seattle Times, Cooking Light, Walking, *and* Fitness Plus.

Rita Stumps

Garipito

for Judy

Lush green leaves edge the branches that form a canopy over the crumbled brown sand inviting my feet to take a first step, then a second, then the thousands it will take me to run below the green cover for the next several miles. I smile when I think about the dappled sun that will accompany me on my journey, sun that will at times fade away almost to nothingness as I travel downhill, deeper into the canyon, sun that will become brighter and clearer as I then work my way back up on the other side. Sun that will illuminate the brilliant yellow, purple, white, red flowers covering the hillsides at this time of year, the time that occurs after the winter rain has gone, before the summer heat has dried everything to the color of straw.

My heart belongs to this time, every Sunday morning, when I face these mountains, this beautiful trail called Garipito, alone. At these times, I also face myself. My mind reconnects to my soul, which restores its ties to the earth around me. I wander alone into this forest primeval, ready to face my deepest demons, emerging on the other side a whole person, saving myself along the way. Saving myself means accepting myself, in spite of what anyone says, in spite of what my own upbringing tells me.

I begin running. My muscles send the familiar signal that tells me they feel tight, tired, and not at all ready for a cross country trek. My mind begs me to go home, go back to sleep, go running another time. It tells me not to think, because thinking hurts, muscle soreness can be soothed by stretching, hot baths, and warm sweatpants, but emotions cause pain that has to be faced directly.

My friends who don't run always ask me what I think about, what occupies me as I wander along the trails. Sometimes music, I reply, sometimes a song comes into my head, and I reflect on the lyrics. Sometimes just nature herself, I add, citing times when I've seen deer, coyotes, rattlesnakes, rabbits, skunks. And sometimes, I think of problems, coming to terms with them along the way. I have faced the major challenges of my life here.

I haven't realized it, but already I've headed perhaps a mile downhill, my head tuning out my legs, my mind wandering as it usually does. Dust kicks up behind me as my legs keep up a steady, gentle rhythm. Occasionally, pebbles scatter as well, and slippery leaves flick into the air, striking my ankles, then settling into new patterns on the ground behind me. Branches gently brush my arms and legs, and occasional mustard flowers leave small golden stains on my shirt. My breath settles into its familiar three-beat rhythm, in-out-out, in-out-out, in-out-out, keeping a staccato pace with my feet, one-two-three, one-two-three, one-two-three. At one time, several years ago, words ran through my head, keeping the same beat, I am not, I am not, I am not. I am not a lesbian.

I was determined not to be a lesbian at that time, and had done everything I could to deny it. After all, how could I, a woman in a heterosexual marriage, possibly be gay? Never mind my reasons for marrying, to fit in, fulfill my family's expectations, resign myself to the fate that seemed to make everyone around me so happy. I had no personal control, except in one area. As an anorexic controls her body through obsessive dieting, so I controlled the only aspect of my life I could, my only time alone, my precious time spent in the hills. Running those many miles helped me deny who I really was; by controlling speed and distance, I could control myself, and keep the secret I swore never to reveal to anyone, especially to myself.

Going into the forest brings back that painful time of hiding. I ran into the forest in my head, hid my soul inside the branches of my mind, tucked my emotions into an inner confusion of the colors and textures of my everyday life, a life that did not, could not, would not include loving a woman. The trail got deeper and darker as I hid among the increasingly dense foliage. I continued downward, and the light began to fade; coolness surrounded me, and I came closer to an ultimate despair, one that did not exclude the idea of suicide.

My trail also has a bottom. At that point, a small river meanders through the foliage and over the trail. It mostly trickles its way along, but after a strong spring rain becomes deep and rough, a challenge to cross. Many times I've slipped while trying to step carefully from rock to rock, unintentionally soaking my feet. I spent years avoiding immersion in life, years running and hiding, and ultimately bathing anyway, falling into myself. I changed my life out of desperation, out of a desire to leave what I had settled into, the deep unhappiness, teetering on the unstable edges of my identity, crashing into my newfound lesbian identity almost overnight. I left behind life as I knew it, marriage, money, the illusion of the happy wife. I risked losing everything, my solid, stable life, my family, my friends.

I remember very well the night I finally talked to my husband. I don't usually drink alcohol, but that night it took two beers and several hours of crying before I could face him and talk to him, before I could confide in him the reason for our failed marriage.

I was lucky, because almost immediately the trail began to go uphill. He turned to me and said, "Now I understand," and we talked for the first time in months. I lost a husband but gained a friend that night, one who supported me in spite of the pain I caused him.

And so it is with my running trail. As I cross the river, safely this time, I almost immediately notice the trail leading gently uphill, almost unnoticeably at first, then slightly more steeply, becoming difficult at times, easing off a bit at others.

Traveling uphill gets easier along the way. At first muscles strain and thighs ache; breathing hurts. My legs and lungs catch up, however; I eventually settle into a rhythm that gets more comfortable, relaxing even, and my body ceases to strain.

Coming out was the same way. I'll never forget that first visit to the therapist, crying when I spoke those words for the first time— "I'm gay." She handed me tissues, asking me, "What are you going to do about it?" With her help, I made it to my first lesbian rap session. I was terrified. I sat in a chair, part of a circle of people yet very definitely an outsider, as others spoke I only listened, afraid to open my mouth. It took a few visits before I could open up. When I finally did, the support I received overwhelmed me. I met many friends through that group, including, eventually, the woman with whom I now share my life.

Pleasant surprises greeted me along the way of my personal journey, just like on my trail. I see the first signs of flowers, tiny purple blossoms nestled close to the ground. I have to keep my eyes moving and alert to see them, so subtle and shy are they. These small gifts resemble the small gifts from my support group, a cartoon drawn for me by one woman, a telephone number given to me by another, telling me to call if I needed to talk, just to talk, nothing else.

More flowers appear as I reach higher ground. Now come big, leafy bushes with bright red blooms. They still prefer the darker hillsides, too much sun would fade them, dry them out. My first lesbian steps were like that, too, bold steps, but quietly made in the comforting shadow of groups of friends, a meal at a restaurant, a hike with an all-women's walking club, a local film or lecture.

As I journey along the last mile or so, I feel an incredible lightness, reflected by the growing sun around me, and the knowledge that I will soon reach the end of the trail, and finish my run. My steps get more confident, my body rushes a little more, excited because of the inevitability of reaching my goal. Bright orange and yellow fields overwhelm everything else on the hillsides. They announce their presence brashly, boldly, daringly.

Rita Stumps, a long-distance runner since 1984, has participated in numerous races of various distances, including five marathons. She grew up in Germany and the United States, and now lives in North Hollywood, California, with her life partner and two cats.

Irene Reti

Grandma's Marathon

Six months after my grandmother's death, I ran my first marathon, and that marathon was called Grandma's. My grandmother was not a runner, but she believed in challenges and she believed in me. "Go ahead. Always go ahead," she would advise me. It was her sharp, accented voice that I heard when I awoke in the early morning light. And somehow the completion of this marathon, an event in which I was fully present in my body and spirit, running through the world full of passion and self-confidence, was a vital milestone in my healing from my grandmother's death.

The sun rose over Lake Superior, a red ruby over black water. Overexcited, I hadn't been able to sleep for most of the night, but that morning as I slipped on my grape-colored Lycra shorts and rubbed Glide under my armpits and between my legs to prevent chafing, I felt powerful, ready to run.

I drank two glasses of water and ate a banana. Two other women runners and I drove down Park Point, a four-mile-long sand spit that juts out into Lake Superior and is separated from the rest of Duluth by the Aerial Lift Bridge, which lifts to allow shipping traffic to pass from the Duluth Harbor into the rest of the lake. We drove over the bridge and boarded the yellow school buses that would take us the twenty-six miles up scenic Highway 61 to the start at Two Harbors.

I had drunk a steady supply of water the day before and that morning. I had been warned about running in the humid Midwest, the dangers of dehydration. Ten minutes after the bus left Duluth I was miserable. I had to pee. Desperately. The ride up the coast became an exercise in bladder torture. Ironically, it was those moments on the bus that would be the hardest moments of my marathon experience.

It was only 6:15 A.M. when the yellow school bus let us out in a huge green field and we made a mad dash for the Porta Pottis. My caution in prehydrating would pay off later. It turned out to be the hottest, most humid Grandma's marathon in the twenty-one-year history of the race. At 7:30 A.M. when the race began the temperature was already in the high sixties and the humidity was 98 percent. By the end of the race it would be eighty-one degrees.

I smeared sunscreen on my freckled shoulders. I was being daring and wearing a blue and white Santa Cruz Track Club racing singlet. Brave because my redhead's complexion was not used to the sun and my shoulders are pale.

I was standing in the field. People were stretching, tying and retying their shoes, popping Advil. I felt completely calm.

It had been a long journey for me to that marathon. I had never seen myself as athletic. Gym was a series of traumatic experiences—of volleyballs that hit me on the head, softballs that I ducked to miss, tennis rackets that slipped out of my hands. My most treasured athletic memories were of bowling, the solidity of hard black balls that fit my small fingers, the black and green shoes, the satisfying crash of the ball knocking down pins, the magic of the machine that endlessly reset them.

I was almost always the last girl picked for teams. Gym shorts never fit my wide hips. I hid my flat chest, getting dressed behind a white plastic shower curtain in the locker room, soaking my socks rather than reveal my body. I did not think of this short, round Jewish body as the body of a runner, an athlete. I had thought of myself as shy and uncoordinated, bookish and awkward, clumsy and clueless.

And yet I was a strong girl. I had muscles in my legs. I was the girl who walked two miles to high school each way, past the secret canopies under deodora trees, counting the heads of spindly palms in the gray Los Angeles sky. I walked fast and strong, the HOLLY-WOOD sign above me. I learned to walk faster and faster and perfected the art of reading while walking, knew just how far I had between each cross street, each mailbox or lamppost.

I was also the girl who climbed mountains. By age seven I was scaling manzanita-studded scree slopes with my parents. I hiked up ten-thousand-foot Lassen Peak. By age fourteen I was an avid back-packer, taking ten-day, seventy-mile trans-Sierra trips, climbing ser-rated Mount Whitney, the highest mountain in the continental United States.

I had only been running seriously a year and a half. My early forays into running were brief flirtations. Once I loved a tall woman with blond ringlets and high cheekbones. It was 1980 and she led me on prancing jaunts on twisting redwood-lined paths. I would have followed her anywhere but she was terrified of my love for her and ran out of my life. Eight years later my friend Leslie led me on a few gasping runs through Santa Cruz. Leslie was a runner in high school, setting her school's record for the mile. She's completed three marathons. Leslie talked and I sucked air next to her, utterly nauseated. We ran one mile. It was not fun.

Six years later Shoney and I ran along the ocean. Shoney had recently developed an enthusiasm for running. I owned no running bra and ran with my hands over my chest, protecting my breasts. We ran to the surfer statue and back. I sweltered in sweatpants but felt exhilarated when we finished two miles. We did this for two weeks. Then Shoney developed a stress fracture in her leg, and that scared me away from running for over another year.

In December of 1995, Valerie Jean, my lover of eight years, left me. After so many years of adapting to her moods and needs, I was living alone for the first time in my life. I fell in love with my house with woodstove, loft, and view of the sea. I began to hear my inner voice, stayed up late at night reading and talking to friends, writing. I also looked at the path winding along the sea, felt my legs yearn. I want to do something to strengthen my confidence in my body, I thought. Maybe I *could* run?

I had started slowly, began by running on winding dirt paths for twenty minutes through Lighthouse Field, the state park across the street from my house. I enjoyed the company of golden retrievers, monarch butterflies, poppies and lupine, sculpted Monterey pine.

After a week of this I ventured out onto the path above the ocean, and ran a few blocks along the golden sandstone cliffs above rocks crowded with barking sea lions. The first time I ran the mile to a huge cypress tree I was ecstatic. A few weeks later I ran to the state park and back, a three-mile round trip. I came home, climbed up into my loft, and cried with happiness.

In February 1996 I signed up for my first 10K race, a benefit for the Battered Women's Shelter in Monterey, California. It seemed appropriate that my first race was for a strong feminist cause. What I remember about that first race was the spit, how I ran through the spit-marked pavement of a community of runners and didn't mind. That spit marked a magical collectivity, my membership in a new society. We were somehow one being, running down that path by Lover's Point, panting and spitting and pounding, past jumbled granitic rocks, fog, sea otters and sea lions, the cypresses muted in the mist.

I signed up for race after race that spring and summer. The Clam Chowder Chase, where I discovered I loath running on sand. The Race for Knowledge, along my beloved cliffs, which benefited the public library. The Firecracker Race, which I ran the day I learned my grandmother was dying. I ran through hot summer grass, holding my arm against my aching ribs, which had dislocated in an old car accident.

Somewhere between all these races and my evening runs on the cliffs in the lengthening daylight, I became a runner. My body began telling me to run when I hadn't in a few days. I began to fidget, to feel less confident. I stopped feeling like I *should* run. I *wanted* to run!

Friends began to notice changes in my body. "You're walking differently, holding yourself differently," they praised. "You seem more confident, stronger somehow." I accepted their compliments shyly, felt proud. I could sense the changes in myself but wasn't sure if it was the running or living alone for the first time, being free of a relationship in which I'd given up my power.

"Hey, you've lost weight!" The women at work meant well but I felt uncomfortable with their "compliments." I have struggled my whole life to love my body and their comments brought up complex feelings in me, as had my own weight loss. Fat women are beautiful. Wasn't my body beautiful at its larger size?

In October of 1996 I had run my first half marathon through the giant redwoods of Humboldt County along the Eel River. I ran strong and slow through green filtered light, took good care of myself. The air was cold and fresh. I sped up during the second half of the race, finished the second half faster than the first. After the race my soul was filled with an impressionistic blur of muscular legs, river water, burnished fall meadows, hollow trees along a shadowed road.

My race time was 2:22, very slow. But although I am competitive in other aspects of my life, in running I miraculously don't put pressure on myself. I challenge myself, wanting to feel fitter and fitter, but don't compare myself to the other, faster runners. Perhaps as a larger runner I will never be fast. And maybe that's just fine.

As I finished the Humboldt half marathon I had stood in a grove of ancient redwoods, and heard myself say to Shoney, "I want to do a marathon."

The long months of training for the marathon were filled with women. I had run with Katherine, city council member, sixty-four-year-old Amazon. We ran once a week up the coast, through fields of poppies and lupine. By April we had run eighteen miles through the redwoods, a challenging route that includes a five mile hill. Katherine told me stories about city council meetings and the transit district as we ran. I ran with Sue, an intensive care neonatal nurse. Sue was training for the Anchorage Marathon, which is the same day, June 21, as Grandma's. Sue never seemed to run out of breath or bad puns, or poignant stories about the babies she takes care of. I ran with Kay and Shasta on foggy wet mornings through the redwoods. We talked about our struggles to love our bodies, to learn our limits. I ran with Shoney and Jennifer and discussed feminist politics as we loped along the railroad tracks by the river. Kathy and I ran along the shore, discussed writing and relationships. I ran with the women of the Santa Cruz Track Club who gave me encouragement each Wednesday night. All of these women had propelled me toward June 21 and the North Shore of Lake Superior, Minnesota. Their love and faith in me, and watching them meet and surpass their own running goals, had inspired me.

And my trust in my own body had grown. First six miles had seemed like a long run. Then nine miles was a huge accomplishment. This lengthened to thirteen, then eighteen. My arms had grown more muscular. My legs had become firm and strong. On hikes I found myself calmly crossing streams and traversing cliff edges, where before I had shied away, shaking. I completed two twenty-two-mile training runs, one completely alone. Two weeks before the marathon I finished a 5K race with a pace of 8:50 per mile. I was ready for the marathon.

Why out of all the marathons in the country had I picked Grandma's? I could tell you it was because *Runner's World* gave it a rating as one of the top ten marathons in the country. It has a reputation for being mostly flat and for taking good care of the runners, for being a friendly marathon. But really I chose Grandma's because of a woman. I loved a woman that year who called this North Country home. Now she is no longer my lover, but it was her love that had drawn me to these shores, to run along these ancient volcanic cliffs, through these forests of birch and balsam poplar, her love for this lake, for Minnesota, her native land. She spoke to me of ice cliffs, of Indian paintbrush and herring gulls, of thimbleberry and raspberry. In these North Woods wolves and moose still roam through swamps and loons call to their babies across ten thousand lakes. There are dozens of root-beer-colored rivers—French River, Sucker River, Knife River, Lester River. Everything speaks of an abundance of water, the huge bachelor's buttons, the four-foot pink and purple spikes of lupine, the enormous wizened heads of cattails. Even my lover was large, carrying her beautiful, abundant body with grace and confidence.

They say the magnetic spirit of Lake Superior guides the runners of Grandma's Marathon. Lake Superior is the largest of the Great Lakes, holds as much water as the rest of the Great Lakes combined. It takes the sun itself thirty minutes to travel across this lake. No one swims in Lake Superior, even in the summer, because the average temperature is forty degrees. In November and March enormous storms create twenty-foot oceanic waves on the lake, storms that have sunk entire ocean liners over the years.

So this was the immense lake along which I ran. At 7:30 A.M. the gun went off and we seven thousand runners began our journey from Two Harbors to Duluth. I ran in a mad blur of light and shadow, of red and yellow columbine, of pink and purple spikes of lupine along a dark asphalt road. And the lake, the lake in its bed of Precambrian rock drew the runners inexorably southward. In the first mile, I joined the other runners discreetly peeing in an aspen grove by the side of the road. I felt like a small red bear in Lycra shorts, ambling along, hardly racing. At the first-aid station a dozen nine-year-olds in matching red shirts handed out brimming white cups of water. Herring gulls swooped over the narrow road. Three months before this lake had been frozen. My lover had written to me about the wolf who stared in her window farther up this shore.

Wolves. Bear. Moose. Creature of sports drinks and sunscreen, I was hardly one of them, here for a brief season between snow-storms. That day the air was hot and humid, sucking at my pale body. I had never felt myself so clearly made of water, as if my very substance could leak through my running shoes and ebb across the asphalt, simply evaporate into the Minnesota air. My feet ached as they struck the hard road. My shoulders burned. Like my mother, I knew I was of this earth.

And I ran. Pure creature I ran. Past frothing rivers. Past Knife River, Sucker River, French River, Stony Point. Old women cheered by the side of the road. Rural people had set up card tables with oranges and water they handed out to runners as we went by. There were seven thousand of us and I was much closer to the back of the pack than the front, but they were still cheering when I ran by. "Go runners!" "Go 433!" Someone looked at my purple hat and yelled, "Go purple!"

Almost suspended in time, in space, along this largest of lakes, I ran. Far down the coast the Aerial Lift Bridge in Duluth shimmered like a small toy, a distant mirage. Across that bridge was my lover's house. She would be waiting for me at the end of this run. She did not run but she was a strong woman in other ways and I loved this difference between us. I thought briefly of how it would be to hug this woman at the end of my journey.

But she was miles away and what was real was this run, this motion, this North Shore collage of cheers and sweat. The miles flowed by. Nine. Ten. Thirteen. Fifteen. Eighteen. Grandma's Marathon was a hundred shades of green trees—dark fir, poplar, birch, aspen, mountain ash, spruce, red pine, cedar, tamarack, maple, jack pine, alder. Deep brown dragonflies migrated above the runners, followed us toward Duluth.

Grandma's Marathon was rural Minnesota culture, was friendly Scandinavian faces, was signs for Mel's maple-smoked trout, for wild rice at $8.99 a pound, for self-serve worms, for Betty's pies, for Norwegian and Swedish imports. Garden hoses were draped over trees, providing welcome cooling-off fountains.

I ran past houses with stereos playing classical music, a live accordion band, gay boys playing "YMCA." I drank water and sports drink at each aid station, walked through on confident legs. I nurtured myself through this marathon like I'd never nurtured myself through anything. I sucked an orange slice, drank, sponged off my salty cheeks tenderly. I wanted to hold myself, to cheer myself on.

Mile twenty. London Road. The outskirts of Duluth. Midwestern houses with wraparound porches. I passed the man from Atlanta I met at the starting line. "How ya doing?" I asked. "Not so good," he admitted. "But you, you look like you're doing great. Keep it up!" A woman in front of me wore a yellow shirt with dozens of names of women on it. THESE WOMEN DIED OF BREAST CANCER, the shirt said. THIS RUN IS FOR THEM. I began to cry.

Glensheen. A gated mansion where twenty years ago an old woman was murdered in her sleep because someone wanted her money. Mile twenty-three. We entered the commercial district of Duluth. Wendy's. Best Western. Burger King. McDonald's. Only three miles left, the length of my first runs on the cliffs a year and a half before. I pumped my legs as if in a dream. I had no doubts that I would finish that race. Almost everyone I passed was walking by now and many were limping. But I ran, ran even faster down Superior Street, through downtown Duluth, past my lover's office, under skyways and brick buildings, down Lake Avenue. Spectators were screaming, "You're almost there!" I could hear the music in Canal Park.

I put on a final sprint and crossed the finish line. The clock read 4:42. Someone handed me a cup of water. Someone put a medal around my neck and said congratulations. Someone handed me a red rose. Then I was swallowed by the crowd. Only then did I realize how dazed and tired I felt, though I was not in pain. I wandered on wobbly legs in search of something, anything to eat, accosted a guy with a cookie, "Where'd you get that?" I picked up my finisher's T-shirt, discovered a table with bananas and candy bars, gulped some more water, retrieved my bag of clothing from the morning.

I finally found my lover on the deck, still looking for me, her camera pointed at the finish line. Somehow she hadn't recognized me in my running clothes, missed me coming in. She felt bad, but I told her it was okay, what mattered was knowing she would be there. She hugged me hard, sweat and all. "I can't believe you are smiling!" she said.

In that moment of triumph, standing by that vast lake, at the end of my journey, I loved myself entirely, felt absolutely confident and content. I thought about how my grandmother lived her life, surviving and savoring every moment. And I knew I would always carry this moment.

Bettianne Shoney Sien

My Phantom Grandmother

for Louisa 1957

Not in the crevice of sandstone by the river, not behind the rotting barn, not under the glacier rock fence, not jammed into the lightning-cracked oak.

I searched, Grandma, for your legs. I found only wild violets, lily of the valley, arrowheads. She haunts me, my guardian angel, my phantom grandma. Hovers over me in her faded yellow pansy dress. Her wings hiss, "My legs."

On judgment day, they'll rise out of their tiny caskets and re-attach themselves. Grandma too, will rise like the bright cartoon characters on the tarot card. She'll ask for 7-up and pretzels. Her legs will come to her, dancing the polka. They'll waltz to her, in sensible black shoes.

I searched, Grandma. They're not by the marsh where the bloodsuckers covered my legs and the reeds left welts.

When I find her legs I will pull myself up on them; her shadow will shade me from the violent afternoon sun.

"Scratch them for me baby girl," my phantom grandma begs.

I wonder how she lost them. Or were they just gone, like the button on my blue-and-white checked dress. Or the last piece in the puzzle.

"I've lost my legs," she cries, "lost them." How did she get home without them? Ride on a brown and white cow? The back of a Chevy pickup? Or did she phone for help, "Gone. No, not the pigs, my legs." Her accent thick over the phone.

If I find them and open the decaying chest, will they leap like from Pandora's box? Charge ahead, gleeful to run with no more chidren clinging to them like bloodsuckers?

But they keep themselves hidden under the black earth, deep to protect themselves from dogs and other digging animals. Perhaps mushrooms will sprout in a circle to mark that spot. Perhaps they'll root. Grow into strong fat trees. Walking trees with ten thousand legs. Trees that tango. That dip their roots between the fuzzy bursting cattails into the thick marsh water.

I pull the frayed log cabin quilt off and grab her to my cot. I wrap her fingers tightly around my small feet.

"Here they are Grandma. I found them."

Patricia O'Donnell

Early November

Early one morning, early in November, a woman leaves by the back door of her parents' house. She is visiting, from a coast, where waves crash and cities roar, and the air is full of strange tongues and shouting voices. She is not young; her dark hair, flying loose around her, is streaked with gray. Every step she runs reminds her that her body is just recently pulled from sleep, from the forgetfulness and passivity and eternal hope that sleep implies.

This small town is poised on the edge of winter. It is early enough in winter that the air is still clear and brilliant, and there is dew on the grass. Later in the season the dew will be frost, hard and ironic. But she decides, as she runs, that the season is actually late autumn, with the joy, the beauty of an autumn that lingers, reluctant to give way. This moment is a gift. It will soon pass, soon be a memory, and so as she runs she keeps her eyes open wide, and breathes in deeply. To taste this day, this morning, this place.

The air tastes sweet, clear and simple, with simple yearnings, like childhood. She can feel the muscles in her legs, and the slight throbbing in her sinuses. She wants to ignore her body, which demands that it be who she is at this time. She wants to forget it and become part of another time, another body. She has heard that wishing to be someone else is a death wish but she does not wish to be someone else; she wishes to be more herself than she is, she wishes to be the self she has sometimes been. It is a life wish; a wish for more life than she remembers how to live.

She runs through a cemetery, with its winding path and heavy trees. Bones dream beneath her feet. Tree branches lean over her, anxious to drop more leaves than they have. The trees, or the bones, are speaking to her in urgent muttering voices but she out-distances them: this is not the day for that. When she leaves the cemetery she runs on the grass of lawns by the curb. A house on the right, bobbing slowly past, is where she used to play naughty as a child. Every day one summer the girl who lived there would call up and say "Can you come over today." Not understanding that she had a choice, she would say "yes" and walk over heavy of heart. In the bedroom upstairs, a bedroom arranged in an awkward and ungraceful way, with ugly pictures on the walls, the girl would play games she did not want to play. The house is paneled in brown now, and the other girl is grown up and has teenage children. The woman doesn't ever have to go there anymore, yet a part of her is always held in that upstairs room. She looks at the house as she runs past and then turns her eyes up, to the half-naked branches.

Across the highway are houses and memories. They are places she can taste in her mind, always with her even though she cannot remember them, like the memory of a murder, like the first taste of happiness. She is running to go back in time. Some unremembered memory is painful to her. Her sneakers thud and she returns to her muscles, tired and not so young; what is she running for?

The air is cool on her bare arms below the sleeves of the T-shirt. She moved from this town twenty years ago. She grew up here, and will never move back. She feels the darkness of guilt, moving up the back of her thighs, leadening. She also feels a secret food in the air, in the earth that her shoes thump against, in the bodies of the dead giving themselves to the trees. She wants to own this conjunction of feelings, an original patent, but she suspects that feelings are really like gods, or gases, sweeping the earth, partaken of by many. Part of many, not belonging to just one. Held in the bare arms of the trees all the long winter, like wisps of cotton candy, waiting to be dropped on someone, invisible spiderwebs. Or seeping into the tree through the bark, gifts from the dead, running with sap through the veins when the weather warms.

She runs past the diner where the birthday party was held for the girl who made her play naughty. She remembers that she ordered tomato soup at the party, then got sick and threw it up. The memory brings her satisfaction; her body understood her, reflected who she was. She lets her feet take her past the diner, out of town into mystery.

On the right, tall graceful trees, grass still green under the fallen leaves. The park like a dream of graciousness. The place is what she always knew sex could be. The river has not dulled with time; it still glitters. She was a virgin in this park. She thought that once she was no longer a virgin she would be different, would walk or talk or see differently. The day after it happened things looked only a touch different, a slight bit altered. Then she had gone looking for greater changes. This is not all of the world, she had told herself; the world was breaking in explosions of sound and color, just around the corner, ahead of her, elsewhere. Yet now, as she runs beside the river at seven-twenty on a beautiful rich morning in early November, she feels that perhaps this *was* all of the world.

She will be here for two days only. The choices of her life have imposed stringent rules on her. She suspects, once again, the rules are a film over the earth, hanging invisible in trees. When she was younger she thought those rules would not apply to her. She learned that she was not special, that it is all the same. Her feet drag in piles of thick leaves. Time has taken away something, and will take away yet more, and it is valuable and she has still not learned how to appreciate it.

Now her arms are stupid and useless, and she slows until she nearly stops. Father McGowan at catechism class used to tell them they were all special. But his eyes were distant, filmed behind his glasses with sadness and she thought he couldn't see her. She sits on the bank of the river, tired and heavy, and looks at the water that flows like a melody. Everyone stops running at times to rest heavily on grass on the bank of a river. Things are to be lost; time takes them away, or we take them away from ourselves because we think we can't use them anymore. They are lost except for a moment, when we come close to what was, when we feel the memory of something lost deep in our bodies on a lovely day in early November.

She has rested by the water long enough. The river's movement is inspiring, its flash and ripple. And soon this weather will be gone; soon days like this, with these kinds of colors, will be only a memory.

Color is all over, from the sick orangey red soup to the leaves, which still have a zingy loud color here and there they like to shout against the sky. And the sky itself is a steady and self-reliant blue, not hesitant. On the ground are enormous brown leaves: she is at this moment running through the biggest brown leaves she has ever seen. She picks one up. It must be maple, but brown and sturdy. Homeless people where she lives could collect these leaves, use them for blankets.

She runs through the trees to where she sees the old shelter house, centered on the spot where it belongs. She recognizes this feeling of things being exactly right from her childhood. Adults know the tentativeness of things, and know how easily mistakes are made. The shelter of her childhood is secure as sweet milk, warm as skin.

Then a swing set, old-fashioned, of solid oak. She remembers when the world started to tilt, became ragged and dangerous around the edges. Junior high picnic, a walk in the woods. A shy boy picked wild violets and she tucked them into the pocket of her blouse, just over the new woman-curve. The evening of that day when she looked back the picnic appeared luminous, glowing and bright as a split-opened heart of watermelon, and it seemed to her that this is what the rest of her life would be like.

She drives her body like a car down the park road, winding to the dam. She picked Paul up from his parents' house on Easter day because she was in love with him, and drove with him to the dam. The sky was fracturing open, and there was something that caught the breath in her throat. Paul wrote with a stick in the sand at the edge of the river—"Jesus was here."

She slows as she runs toward the dam. Water pours over the rocks of the small dam, only a few feet high. Kids used to walk across it to be brave, to impress. When Paul wrote "Jesus was here" it seemed the truth. He was standing next to her on the bank, and his skin was very pale and white and his legs were skinny. And his eyes glanced at her, then away to the sky. He was alive beside her, on a cool day in early spring.

What she feels when she remembers this is a feeling like all the others, sucked into the sap of trees to find a home in the human breast next to violets, but she knows it is a sap more rare. It is water flowing and skin and colors against the sky. Now Paul is gone and their child, hers and Paul's, sleeps on the West Coast in her dorm room, tossing and turning, dreaming of running.

At the dam's edge she stops, panting, her forehead wet with sweat. She bends down, picks up three pebbles and tosses them: one for her, one for Paul, one for their child. One for childhood, one for youth, one for now. Their splashes are tiny, inaudible. She laughs, riding an upsurge, a flash from the sun making its way above the trees, and is on her way.

Patricia O'Donnell teaches fiction writing in the B.F.A. program in creative writing at the University of Maine at Farmington. Her fiction has appeared in The New Yorker, The Agni Review, The North American Review, Short Story, *and other places.*

Anna Viadero

Running for My Life

At eight years old, living outside Chicago, I was the one to run the high-trafficked city mile to our local bakery where two kind women risked their jobs to help feed our large "financially challenged" family. They'd call my mom several times a week at minutes before closing and I'd be the one to run to get the bag of day-old baked goods and bring it home for our family of six kids and four adults to divide. My distance running began with those bakery runs.

When my grandma fell sick I'd be the one to sprint to get our neighbor, Dr. O'Hara, who lived a block down. I'd pull and drag him as though I could run a fat, fifty-year-old cardiologist along with me. He was always patient and kind with me those days while he provided gratis aid.

Working at the Walgreen's drug store in high school I got out after nine—after the buses had stopped, so I had to run home because our family couldn't afford a car. I ran through the bus terminal and taxi stand, under whichever train bridge was best lit that night. I ran on the grass between the sidewalk and the street because I was afraid someone might be hiding in the manicured bushes near the church.

I ran after Larry, an eighth-grader in my Catholic grade school, closed the switchblade he had held to my ten-year-old chest in a foolish act of terrorism. I was on my way to church for Good Friday mass when he pulled me into an alley. When he let me go I ran with his laughing in my ears and Dr. O'Hara's daughter's hand-me-down skirt wrestling with my thighs.

I ran from Rita, a wicked girl in my new public middle school the year the Catholic school refused to pick up my family's tuition anymore. I ran after she whispered to me everyday in last home-room that she and her friends would kick my ass outside right after school. The dismissal bell would ring and I would bolt down the stairs and out, books wedged close to my body, sprinting up one short hill and six blocks over to the synagogue whose doors were always open. Then I'd walk the three blocks home. I ran without thinking, my breathing echoing in my ears. I ran so blindly from Rita that once I hit an iron grate in school near my exit door and passed out cold. I woke in the nurse's office and begged her not to call my mother, just drive me to the synagogue and I'd be safe.

I ran in high school because I didn't fit in. I ran at the YMCA because I wasn't supposed to. Only fat, old, rich men, our town's bankers and lawyers, were supposed to run there. They'd take off work at three and come jog or walk the twenty-four laps to that elevated mile. I came into their space one day in Converse basket-ball shoes and ran between and around them for months until I made that track my own. When I earned enough baby-sitting money to buy men's running shoes I burned those men off the track. I timed myself only once for one mile. Five minutes flat. I never ran that fast again.

I ran when boyfriends in high school said I shouldn't—that I was getting too sinewy and thin.

I ran the year my sister and I starved ourselves in the name of beauty. I ran dizzy and wasted until my body broke out in bruises. I promised never to hurt myself like that again.

In college in southern Illinois. I ran and wondered why but never stopped running. I ran for myself. My only team. I ran sidewalks and cornfields and tracks alone.

At another college in Chicago I taught a handsome young man how to put one foot in front of the other. We ran in ice and snow almost sliding into Lake Michigan under the winter moon. That man I married.

I had two little boys with him and they both love to run: one in circles around the basement when it's bad outdoors, the other in short bursts between the trees in our forested yard in any kind of weather.

When my boys were old enough, I took them to the hills of their New England home and watched them breathe the raw power of running. I saw them revel in its freedom. I saw how running for my children is pure joy. So many times in my life it was a necessity.

It might seem strange, but I'm glad I got sidelined. God gave me good legs and I've used and depended on them for years. It took a back injury last year (an injury that grew from taking my body for granted and pushing it too hard) to slow me down enough to appreciate all the places running has taken me. My injury has given me pause. It's let me contemplate the power of my running;

how that power has brought me successes and safety; how running has moved me forward—pulled and shaped me. I've had a chance to look at where I've been and, inspired by this reflection, to imagine all the places my two legs have yet to take me.

Anna Viadero is a writer living in Montague, Massachusetts. Her work has appeared in Women's Words, Earth's Daughter, The Berkshire Review, The Sun *and others. She has read her work on WFCR, public radio from Amherst, Massachusetts..*

Judyth Hill

Running through Fear

A woman runs in pines, in snow.
breath catching in her throat.
It's cold, cold
and clouds part at her feet, suddenly eye level.
She's running.
Running from the business of business, from loss
from checkbooks, a balance of loss, anxious deposits,
and withdrawals of lack.

She's lacking.
She's lacking in time, lacking in money.
She's running in steamy puffs of visible air
and doesn't know how much poverty it takes
to screw in a lightbulb.

She's praying.
She's thanking God for this road where this summer
she saw four deer, and now,

there is always the possibility of deer,

forever a chance to know swift flight and soft fur

slipping over hills.

She's praying, running and praising, *Modah Ani*.

She's grateful.

Grateful for the wind that plays the boughs,

a Corelli of winter, a Bach of lifting and moving on.

She's running.

Running in a world that's white,

that starts over daily

without the carried negative balance,

without the fear in the mailbox,

without the lack.

She's running.

Her thighs ache in the stretch and contract,

blood pulsing, and she's grateful

and lacking

and running

and praying

in cold snow and the chance of seeing deer disappear into forest.

Judyth Hill is a writer, performer and teacher of poetry. She is the author of three books of poetry, and is widely anthologized. She is the director of literary projects for New Mexico Arts, the state's art agency. Her cookbook with poetry and essays, The Dharma of Baking: Recipes from the Chocolate Maven, *was published by Celestial Arts Press in Berkeley, California She was described by the* St. Helena Examiner *as "Energy with skin."*